FROM MASCOT TO AGENT AND EVERYTHING IN BETWEEN

JUSTIN R. HUNT

From Mascot To Agent And Everything In Between:
Career guidance from 11 sports executives I met during my journey into sports

Printed in the United States of America.

TABLE OF CONTENTS

PART ONE: MY JOURNEY

PART TWO: ANALYZING DIFFERENT ROLES IN THE SPORTS INDUSTRY

PART THREE: MY ASSESS, DEVELOP, IMPLEMENT APPROACH TO NETWORKING AND YOUR NETWORKING PLAN

PART ONE: MY JOURNEY

INTRODUCTION

Like most kids growing up, I loved sports. I wanted to be a professional athlete. At the age of 16, I was 5'4" on a good day, 130 pounds soaking wet, and had the athletic prowess of an obese politician. Naturally, given my physique at the time, my path to becoming a professional athlete was clear. A jockey.

My five-inch "growth spurt" at the age of 18 ruled out that possibility. Despite this list of physical attributes that made it virtually impossible for me to become a professional athlete, I was still determined to be involved in sports. So I turned to the next best thing…sports business. From that day forward, I shifted my focus to becoming a sports agent.

I made this decision prior to the release of *Jerry Maguire* and the publication of Drew Rosenhaus' book *A Shark Never Sleeps*. I made this decision without understanding the politics of professional sports organizations. I didn't have the familial connections that so many people rely on to make a name for themselves in the industry. My father was in sales; my mother was a language arts teacher. As a high school student, I had this idea that I wanted to be a sports agent. But I had no idea how to get there.

After high school, I remained committed to becoming a sports agent. I received my B.B.A in finance, obtained my law degree, and pursued my Masters of Sports Administration from Ohio University. I worked in the San Francisco 49ers' front office as a salary cap administrator and subsequently led the football division for Sterling Sports Management, a mid-sized sports agency. I passed the NFLPA's player agent certification exam and had one of my clients drafted in the 5th round of the 2013 NFL Draft, my first season as an NFL agent. I've negotiated player contracts with a cumulative value of over $15 million dollars.

Similar to my decision to become a sports agent, I committed to writing this book prior to working in sports and well before becoming a certified NFL agent. I traveled across the country in pursuit of my first position in sports and met fascinating people along the way. At the time, my intent was to write a book based on my early career in sports. I wrote down what I did and critiqued the path that I decided to take towards getting my first job in sports. Over time, I built strong relationships with prominent executives, and the premise of my book evolved.

I am qualified to talk about building a strong network and obtaining your first job in sports; I accomplished both of these things. But what I am not qualified to talk about are the myriad positions available in the sports industry. I couldn't possibly teach you how to become president or general manager of a sports franchise. I never pursued these positions. More importantly, I never held these positions. But members of my network could. As a result, my book transitioned from a biography of my life into a collaboration among sports executives holding 11 different positions across the Big Four.

I traveled the country and met with each contributor. We had dinner, attended sporting events, or in some instances, both. I learned exactly what it took for them to become the position they held during the production of this book. In doing so, I wanted to provide you with a snapshot of their careers and identify ways to obtain those particular positions. I left it up to my contributors to tell you how to become their successor.

Everything I've accomplished thus far in my career is the result of working hard, but I found out early in my career that hard work alone simply isn't enough. You need a strong network. *An identifiable group of professionals sharing common interests and professional pursuits that is willing to help you succeed.*

Over the course of my journey into the sports industry, I learned that the key to networking is *how* and *why* you approach these individuals. And most importantly, *when* you approach them. I want to help you understand how to network effectively and position yourself to obtain the job that you want.

I understand the value of a strong network now, but I didn't always. Initially, I assumed that my passion for sport and desire to become an agent would carry the day. I first realized that I needed a concrete, thorough plan of attack to make my dreams come to fruition after I auditioned as Rufus.

My tenure as a graduate student was set to expire following the 2010 Ohio Bobcats' Spring Football Game. Twenty minutes before game time, the individual slated as the mascot Rufus for the annual Rufus Run cancelled, sending the students of our program scurrying to find a replacement. Recognizing this as the perfect opportunity to illustrate my passion for sport, I volunteered.

In this capacity, I was required to dance and operate in a fashion shockingly consistent with my mannerisms at the local pub on a Friday night. My role concluded with a 100-yard race with numerous children determined to beat Rufus in the 85-degree heat. This experience provided a moment of clarity unlike any other up until this point in my life. To this day, I am not sure if it was the impending heat stroke or the five-year-old kid humping my leg, but at that moment, two things became clear to me: (1) I wanted out of this damn suit, and (2) I was determined to become an accomplished professional in the sports industry. I needed a plan to get there.

Shortly after my audition as Rufus, I graduated from my master's program without a job in sports. I was qualified from an educational standpoint, yet I had minimal success even learning of vacant positions in the area of my interest, which at the time was the NFL salary cap. The passion that I had for sports didn't automatically translate to a job immediately following graduation. But I eventually got there using my ASSESS, DEVELOP, IMPLEMENT approach to networking outlined in Part Three.

The path into the sports industry is difficult and, in the absence of a strong network, virtually impossible to navigate. I've experienced the individual highs and the individual lows in the industry, and through them all, the solution to every problem and the catalyst to every accomplishment was my network. It positioned me for my role as a salary cap administrator with the San Francisco 49ers. It led to my emergence as a young agent in an incredibly competitive field. This book is a product of my sports network. And I'm certain that my next career endeavor will involve individuals comprising my network.

So how did I do it? How did a high school student aspiring to become a sports agent build a strong enough network to accomplish this and much more? I can trace my involvement in the industry back to a single phone call that shaped my path into the industry. As for how I did it, we need to go all the way back to that phone call with Kevin Abrams.

1

IT ALL STARTED WITH A PHONE CALL

I arrived in Athens, Ohio, in 2009 to pursue my Masters of Sports Administration. Ohio University boasted its reputation as the number one Sports Administration graduate program in the country and its extensive sports network. I received my copy of Ohio's alumni directory almost immediately upon my arrival. Institutions of higher learning use these alumni directories as a recruiting tool to attract promising, up-and-coming professionals in the industry. This directory not only highlights the accomplishments of previous students, but it also helps place current students throughout the industry. I put mine on my bookshelf, gathering dust.

My perception was that my education and scholastic accomplishments would lead to a job. Looking back now, boy, was I wrong.

I eventually began flipping through page by page, taking time to digest the names of the alumni that graduated from the very program I was in the process of completing. While my ultimate goal was to become an NFL agent, I identified steps I should take in the process of becoming a sports agent that would give me a competitive advantage over other agents. One such step was to spend time in an NFL front office.

This quick scan of the directory revealed several prominent executives in sports, and, since my interest was the NFL, my focus gravitated towards the executives currently working for NFL clubs. I came across Kevin Abrams, the current Assistant General Manager for the New York Giants. He was responsible for negotiating player contracts, among other things, for the New York Giants.

I sent Kevin an email to introduce myself and hopefully schedule a call. His office line was listed in the directory, but I wanted to be courteous of his time and get the most out of my call if he were willing to speak. He agreed to speak with me.

I wanted to be sure to take full advantage of this opportunity to speak with a leading executive in professional sports. I conducted research and wrote down a list of questions relevant to his area of the New York Giants' organization. How do you anticipate the new Collective Bargaining Agreement will impact future contract negotiations? How did your experience at the Management Council, the NFL's equivalent of a Club's salary cap department, help you land your current job? And how can I position myself to secure a position as a salary cap analyst upon graduation? The impression I intended to give was that I was prepared and more than just a graduate student looking for a job.

I dialed the number, waited for the ring tone, and finally heard a voice at the other end. I asked to speak with Kevin Abrams, even though he provided me with his direct line!

Although I was nervous at first, I was able to build credibility with Kevin thanks to the research I conducted. I understood how the salary cap was calculated, which contracts counted towards the overall salary cap figure and specific nuances in the CBA that teams used as leverage during contract negotiations. I gained more confidence as the call progressed and asked questions I wouldn't have asked at the beginning of the call. Through his answers, I started to learn a lot about the sports industry and, more specifically, my area of interest.

Kevin helped me identify what needed to be done if I wanted to get a job on the operations side of a professional sports franchise. His recommendations included increasing my knowledge of the NFL's salary cap structure calculated under the CBA and connecting with the appropriate individuals.

He encouraged me to call and connect with current salary cap analysts and general managers in the NFL while I was still in school. Kevin placed significant emphasis on the importance of casting a wide net when attempting to break into the industry. Networking was a concept I knew very little about at the time. After my call with Kevin, I did exactly what he told me to do. I started networking.

I compiled a list of every salary cap analyst and general manager in the NFL. Next to each team, I identified a contact person from Ohio's graduate program that could potentially help me connect with these salary cap analysts and general managers. My goal was to obtain a position as a salary cap analyst upon my graduation from Ohio's program.

I began making some phone calls to these general managers and cap analysts and the list started to dwindle. Some were successful, but the majority of these calls were not. These rejections didn't stop me from connecting with the individuals that were willing to take the time out of their day.

I started making some progress, but I had to use my imagination and find a way to address my lack of knowledge in the industry and my limited network with one action plan. As an attorney, I knew that one of the better ways to establish oneself as an expert in a particular area was by publishing a legal note. So I decided to write one.

A legal note is an extensive article that highlights an impressionable lawsuit whose outcome will have a lasting impact on the parties involved. I decided to cover the then-pending lawsuit between American Needle and the NFL. American Needle was a manufacturer of head wear for the NFL that lost a substantial portion of its business when the NFL granted an exclusive merchandise license to Reebok. Of greater significance was the impact the Court's decision could have on the NFL's revenue distribution, if the Court determined that this exclusive license was in restraint of trade and a violation of antitrust law.

The focus of my note would be the impact that the Court's decision in *American Needle v. N.F.L.* would have on revenue sharing and the salary cap in professional football. A relevant topic, but two problems surfaced when I started writing this note: (1) I knew very little about revenue sharing and the salary cap, and (2) I needed to understand the salary cap in order to get a job in an NFL team's front office.

I began sending emails and following up with phone calls to learn the business model of the NFL and understand the economics of professional sports, with the bonus of adding these individuals to my network. Instead of asking for a job, I asked for assistance with understanding the salary cap and revenue sharing model in the NFL, a passion I presumably shared with these professionals. My response rate skyrocketed.

These individuals started referring me to friends and colleagues currently working in the NFL that understood the complexities of the NFL's economic model. My network became more diverse, and I started to understand the business model of the NFL. My legal note gained some momentum, and I started to posit strategies and outcomes I otherwise wouldn't have understood. I contacted the top law schools offering a legal publication specific to sports to inquire about publication. The University of Virginia's Sports and Entertainment Law Journal published my legal note six months after I decided to write it.[i]

My hope was that this publication would differentiate myself from other candidates once a salary cap position in an NFL front office presented itself. I contacted all 32 NFL organizations to inquire about open positions and, if such a position existed, to submit my résumé for consideration. An overwhelming majority of the clubs did not respond. Most of the teams that did respond did so with a form rejection letter or email.

I received a lead on a potential opening with the San Francisco 49ers in their salary cap department. I spoke with the hiring person in April of 2010 and learned that the organization was leaning towards bringing someone in as a salary cap administrator, but a final decision wouldn't be made until the summer. I waited patiently, but learned a few months later that the 49ers would not be hiring anyone.

My master's program ended in June of 2010. It ended without my being able to secure a position in the NFL, but I refused to fall short of my goal of obtaining a job in an NFL front office before obtaining my agent certification. I was a 26-year-old attorney with mounting school debt. Time was of the essence, or at least that was my mindset.

I went back to the drawing board and crafted a plan that I believed would be my quickest way into the industry. While I made some progress with my network and my knowledge of the industry through the publication of my note, I realized that if I were going to get a job on the operations side in sports, I had to continue to build relationships and work hard in pursuit of such a position while I moved forward with my legal career.

I took a legal job that was anything but sports-related while I continued to form relationships and apply for jobs in NFL front offices. Or at least I thought it was completely unrelated to sports. This legal job was an entry-level attorney position with the international law firm WilmerHale, and I eventually learned that five attorneys currently working in the NFL began their careers at WilmerHale. I developed strong relationships with a few of these attorneys including Alec Scheiner, who went on to become Senior Vice President and General Counsel for the Dallas Cowboys. This experience taught me that there is no harm in taking a "job" while on your journey to establishing your "career."

A portion of my salary was used to finance networking trips with employees of NFL organizations in large cities over my weekends away from the law firm. I perused every sports directory I had access to and sent emails to various sports professionals in the city I was planning to visit. In New York City, for instance, I had breakfast with a New York Knicks' marketing executive (who was previously with the Oakland Raiders and helped me contact Oakland's attorney, Dan Ventrelle), hopped on a train and had lunch with the SVP and General Counsel of the New York Jets and had dinner with a former classmate who was interning with the NFL. I was on a plane home at 7:00 a.m. the next morning.

I attended the NFL Scouting Combine, Super Bowl and any other events that would provide an opportunity to expand my network. A personal contact of mine was able to get me an all access pass to the inside of Lucas Oil Stadium during the NFL Scouting Combine, credentials reserved exclusively for team personnel and media. These trips and experiences helped me build relationships with executives working in sports that had ties to the salary cap or had contacts familiar with the salary cap.

I started asking professionals in a hiring capacity what would make them select one applicant over another should a position

*   *   *   *

Following my position with the 49ers, I had two options: (1) look for opportunities involving the salary cap in another NFL front office, if any opportunities existed, or (2) pursue the agent route. I now had first-hand, front office experience and expertise in the NFL salary cap, so I was fairly certain that my transition over to the agent side of the business was imminent. Yet I still struggled with the fact that this decision wasn't of my own making. I packed what little belongings I had with me in San Francisco and prepared to head home.

My mother agreed to accompany me on my trip back to Ohio. I was excited to learn that she would join me on the car ride back home because her positivity and ability to see the good in everyone and everything was something I needed at that particular moment.

We discussed many different things, the most important of which being my next step and future in the industry. She quickly reminded me of a card that she placed in my Christmas stocking when I was 13 years old. This card, which read, "You Choose Which Party To Attend", was my mother's way of challenging me to view things differently than others. At the time, I gave this very little consideration. This changed over the years.

I started thinking about this phrase when I was rejected by Ohio University, denied admissions to the majority of law schools and stripped of a position in an NFL front office upon graduation. The meaning of this phrase varies depending on the reader. For me, this was my mother's way of encouraging me to see the positives in every situation. I altered this mindset and focused on *turning every negative into a positive.*

This car ride, and more specifically my mother's influence through this slogan, steered me towards all the positives. I leveraged my experience on the team side, the salary cap knowledge that I acquired and the relationships I formed to make a name for myself in pursuit of an opportunity as a sports agent.

For the second time in my short career, I had to rely on my network to help me continue working in sports. Sports agencies

present itself in their organization. One respondent remarked that he would be impressed if someone published a credible note evaluating revenue sharing in the Big Four. The key word in his remark was "credible." If I were going to do this, I needed to make sure that I did it right. I would need a lot of help from executives that understood the revenue structures in the different sports leagues.

One year and hundreds of hours later, I agreed to publish my legal note covering revenue sharing in the Big Four with the University of Texas' Sports Journal.[ii] My publication explained, in a non-legal manner, how to calculate revenue sharing and the salary cap, two mechanisms that determine what professional athletes are paid in a particular sports league. I also projected each individual club's revenues in the upcoming seasons.

This legal note would eventually lead to various interviews with reputable media outlets, such as the *Boston Globe*, *Yahoo Sports* and the *Columbus Dispatch*. I also received a call from the NHLPA during the 2012-2013 lockout, asking me for the documents and financial information I relied upon in making my predictions. No such documentation existed. I projected these calculations based on certain provisions in the NHL's CBA and industry articles on the subject matter.

Despite this recognition and my progress, I had yet to achieve my personal goal of obtaining a position in an NFL front office heading into the NFL lockout.

In May of 2011, amidst the NFL lockout, I received calls from multiple NFL employees informing me that the San Francisco 49ers were looking to hire a salary cap administrator. When I received an email from the hiring executive asking if I would like to be considered for the position, I enthusiastically agreed to submit my information.

The interview process was fairly rigorous. It consisted of three interviews and a player compensation project. This project requested salary cap calculations and other compensation-related data based on the provisions in the CBA. They were testing the applicants' baseline knowledge of the salary cap. The non-salary cap questions were very obscure, and upon my completion of the interviews, I was almost certain I would remain at the law firm. When I started the interviews, the position was full-time. The final offer would be a 3-6 month provisional period with the possibility of a full-time job. Regardless of this change in circumstances, I had every intention of accepting the position if it were offered.

*　　　　*　　　　*　　　　*

The offer came in the form of an email sent from the air following the owners' meeting in Atlanta, Georgia. I was finally presented with the opportunity to work in the National Football League. I accepted the 49ers' offer for an interim position at $10 an hour and left my full-time position with WilmerHale.

I had five days to alert my current employer, pack up my belongings, say my goodbyes, and drive 2,464 miles to Santa Clara, CA, home of the San Francisco 49ers' training facility. I loaded up my Honda Accord and headed for the West Coast. My wife of nine months stayed back in Columbus, Ohio, while I launched my career in the sports industry.

When I arrived at the headquarters for work, I learned that the recent NFL lockout created a backlog of work that couldn't be performed in time with the limited number of staff in the executive offices. The lockout was a work stoppage that resulted from the inability of the owners and players to come to a consensus on a new collective bargaining agreement following the 2010 season, which precluded NFL teams from executing player contracts and managing their salary caps. The lockout broke on July 25, 2011, and teams were immediately permitted to make roster moves and player acquisitions. While these decisions normally occur over a much longer period of time, typically from the beginning of January until the middle of July, the lockout expedited this process.

The organization had a much shorter time period to get everything in order. As a newcomer, I did everything I could to impress anyone that may have been watching. I spent my days performing research and completing assignments. I spent my nights learning the CBA and breaking down individual player contracts to

better understand the market and player compensation terms. myself calculations that both agents and team executives evaluate player deals. I wanted to learn everything I possibl while working in an NFL front office.

This opportunity allowed me to see how teams prepare profile contract negotiations, with Frank Gore and Patrick both extending and restructuring their contracts with the 49er my tenure with the organization. In this role, I was privy to contract information that enhanced my understanding o contracts, the salary cap and the CBA. This information inclu use of supersedes in NFL contracts, the impact that voidabl would have on salary cap calculations and the use of in proceeds to recapture cap space in the event of an injury.

I worked roughly 65 hours a week, even though the organ only paid me for 32. I would return to the office after dinner a until one or two in the morning teaching myself about the sal and valuating different player contracts. I went the extra mile own. This refined and added to my knowledge of the salary c player contracts in the months leading up to the 2011 regular se

The work that had been created by the lockout was com and I was laid off during the 2011 regular season. That par morning, I woke up as an employee in the front office professional sports team. That afternoon, I was unemploye 2,464 miles from my wife and family.

My time in the 49ers' front office, albeit limited, taug many important lessons about the organization (micro-level) a sports industry (macro-level). This experience taught me cutthroat the sports industry could be and reaffirmed that being connected in the sports industry is very important. This, more any other lesson, shaped my career early in my profession. Wit in mind, I prepared to head back east to Columbus, Ohio.

rarely hire agents without an impressive book of business. Aside from being an unpaid intern and paying your dues, the best way into the business as a sports agent is to identify an opportunity and create the demand. It also doesn't hurt to provide cheap labor.

I felt as though I had a lot to offer an existing firm. I had an undergraduate degree in finance, a law degree with a focus on tax and business planning, a master's in sports administration from the nation's premier program, experience working in an NFL front office, an understanding of the salary cap and player contracts that rivaled that of experienced agents, and a strong network of professionals working for NFL clubs.

I had met various owners of sports agencies over the years, but realistically, I only knew a few of them well enough to approach them about giving me an opportunity. So I floated the idea of a former NFL salary cap professional joining their football group. Most of them turned me down immediately, and some didn't even respond. I knew that I had to remain committed to my vision in order to overcome this initial lack of interest.

I spoke with Jeff Chilcoat, a sports agent I had met in Columbus, Ohio, who also served as my sports law professor while I was in law school. Jeff owned Sterling Sports Management, which primarily focused on professional golfers and baseball players, but I knew that he had had a history representing NFL players. In 2012, his involvement representing current professional football players was limited.

We discussed the different options that would allow me to become certified with the NFLPA and pursue my goal of becoming an NFL agent. Everything made sense. I was a young, emerging professional in the sports industry with team experience, undeniable passion and relentless pursuit. Jeff was an experienced NFL agent with an understanding of the business and contacts in the industry. A combination of the two could prove very successful if utilized properly.

In January 2012, I partnered with Sterling Sports Management and prepared to take the NFLPA's agent certification exam in

Washington D.C. I completed the exam later in the year, and, in October 2012, I was informed that I had passed. I was an NFL agent.

2

BEHIND THE SCENES WITH AN NFL AGENT: MY FIRST SEASON

I poured over a list of college football prospects that I had compiled in preparation for the 2013 NFL Draft. This list was a combination of media lists and articles that had been tweaked after speaking with scouting personnel in the NFL. As a young, emerging NFL agent, I couldn't count on signing elite prospects from football-driven institutions. I had to identify legitimate NFL talent that wouldn't attract as much attention from competing agents. While the 2013 NFL Draft was 11 months away, I needed to start recruiting immediately.

In an attempt to convince these 2013 NFL Draft prospects to sign with me, I made hundreds of phone calls. I traveled an estimated 9,000 miles. I stayed overnight in 12 different cities in 7 different states. I went as far east as New York City and as far west as Shawnee, Kansas. I traveled up north to Madison, Wisconsin, and down south to Elon, North Carolina. I hit a deer. I didn't sign any of those prospects. I returned from a trip to Mexico, dropped my wife off at home, slept four hours, and boarded another plane to Raleigh-Durham. I didn't sign that prospect. I tailgated at two different universities 80 miles apart for two different games on the same day, and then drove four and a half hours back home after the second game. I didn't sign either one of those draft-eligible prospects.

Despite all my efforts, I didn't sign a single client for the 2013 NFL Draft as of December 31, 2012.

"You look too young to have the connections my son will need to make it in the NFL."

This was the last of a string of comments made by a prospective client's mother to me in January of 2013. Her comments made me realize that perhaps I wasn't selling the right things during my recruiting pitch. Looking back on all this rejection I had experienced, I asked myself "Why should these prospects sign with a 28-year-old sports agent with limited experience?" These rejections helped me strengthen my sales pitch by focusing on my experience in an NFL front office and knowledge of the NFL's salary cap. This put me in a better position to sign the next prospect.

I received a lead on a player out of the University of Buffalo named Steven Means. Steven was an incredibly productive defensive end at the University of Buffalo, a member of the Mid-American Conference (MAC). The MAC was perceived as a lesser conference at the time compared to the SEC and the other power conferences.[iii] Steven finished his collegiate career with 186 tackles, 38 tackles for a loss and 22 sacks. His statistics alone suggested that he could play at the next level. Unfortunately, stats don't always translate to success in the NFL. I conducted my own due diligence and gathered as much feedback as I could from scouts and talent evaluators I had worked with in the NFL, relying on their advice to help me identify potential NFL prospects. If I were going to make it in this business, it would be by signing these "diamonds in the rough."

These scouts indicated that Steven was an in-between player, where teams could utilize him as a defensive end or an outside linebacker, depending on the defensive front. I had to answer questions like could he drop back in space if a team wanted to use him as an outside linebacker in a 3-4 scheme? Did he have the speed-to-power combination necessary to be an outside pass rusher? How was his pass rush technique? A few scouts assured me that Steven could do these things and could likely play at the next level.

I made the five-hour drive northeast with Jeff Chilcoat to meet with Steven and his parents in Buffalo, NY. We told them why it made sense for Steven to sign with Sterling Sports. I had the drive of a hungry agent determined to succeed with experience working in an NFL front office combined with the experience of an established agency.

It was a very productive meeting, but we left without obtaining Steven's signature on the Standard Representation Agreement (SRA). The SRA is the contractual document signed between an

NFL prospect/player and an agent that commences the player-agent relationship. It was a tough pill to swallow. I thought to myself, "Did I really just make another 10 hour drive and fail to sign my first client?" There was still a chance he would sign with us, but getting the ink on the paper is much easier at the point of sale.

Heading back on Interstate 80 one mile outside Buffalo, I received a call from Steven. He informed me that something had fallen out of my bag and that he found it next to where my bag was sitting in his apartment. It appeared to be something electronic; he assumed it was for my computer. A bit perplexed, we turned around to pick up what Steven had described as a computer part. I knocked on the door and Steven greeted us with a big smile. There was no missing computer part. Steven had signed the SRA!

Instantaneously, it all became worth it. The travel. The rejection. The countless hours of recruiting. At that point, this one signature justified it all. My dream became a reality. I was officially a sports agent with a client.

A few days later, I signed Josh Kline, an offensive guard out of Kent State University. Similar to Steven, I obtained as much scouting feedback as I could on Josh. The general consensus was that Josh could play at the next level. Steven and Josh were graded as priority free agents, which means teams view them as potential contributors but don't feel they are draftable. In my first year as a certified agent, I signed two clients that had a chance to be drafted and could compete for a position on a 53-man roster in the NFL. I couldn't have been more excited to get to work for them.

Every day I worked to attract the attention of NFL clubs and increase my clients' chances of playing football in the NFL. I started by making phone calls to their college coaches. They can help an agent understand his or her clients' strengths and weaknesses and identify areas for improvement as they prepare for the NFL Draft. They also serve as a direct link between the NFL scouts that visit the various schools and agents. These coaches and faculty in the athletics department can help an agent understand what clubs are interested and what clubs are not.

Once I established a good rapport with members of the coaching staffs, I worked with faculty to understand my clients' character and establish that they have the intangibles that NFL clubs look for in a prospect. NFL scouts have total access to a prospect's film. They know if he can play the game. What they don't have is a direct connection with the information that establishes he has football intelligence, or even more important, the ability to lead. My job was to help NFL teams understand this about my clients.

Later in the pre-Draft process, I made every attempt to get my clients an invite to one of the four primary all-star games that highlight the strengths and abilities of draft-eligible prospects. NFL scouts and personnel staffs flock to the Senior Bowl, the East-West game, Texas v. Nation, and the NFLPA Collegiate Bowl in the month of January. Josh Kline was not invited to play in any of these all-star games. As his agent, it was incumbent upon me to do my best to make sure he received an invite. Players get injured, players drop out of the game, but regardless of the reason, I had to make sure that my client(s) became the replacement. After weeks of phone calls, I finally was able to get Josh an invite to Texas v. Nation.

Lastly, I made phone calls to all 32 clubs in an attempt to increase my clients' exposure to these clubs. NFL clubs have limited opportunities to evaluate prospects in person following the college football season. The first opportunity is the all-star games mentioned above. Second, NFL scouts gather in Indianapolis, Indiana, every February to attend the NFL Scouting Combine. The Combine offers an opportunity for NFL prospects fresh out of college to showcase their skills. This is an invite-only event that is very difficult, if not impossible, for agents to manipulate. Third, the majority of college programs host a pro day for their athletes to display their skills in front of any NFL scouts that choose to attend. The fourth and final opportunity to evaluate college prospects entering the NFL Draft is private workouts and visits to a club's facility.

The individual clubs in the NFL spend the final month of the pre-Draft process conducting private workouts at a specific institution's facility and coordinating visits at the club's facility. Clubs are permitted to invite up to 30 prospects to visit their facility and conduct medical tests (Top 30 visit). If a club elects to visit the institution to conduct a private workout, no such limitation exists. They can visit as many prospects as they want to get a closer look. I called every club over and over again to schedule these workouts or Top 30 visits.

At the close of the pre-Draft process, Steven Means had three Top 30 visits and six private workouts. Josh Kline had three Top 30 visits and five private workouts. I took a proactive approach and made sure that if there were any interest on behalf of the club, it would be easy to get them information on my clients and schedule a workout. The athlete representation business is too cutthroat to sit back and wait for these opportunities to occur.

I used this information to gather a list of the Top 10 clubs that had expressed interest in my clients. I cross-checked this list with my list that established a club's need at my clients' positions. If either one of my clients slipped out of the Draft, my job would be to help him choose the club whose needs matched his interest.

I advised both of my clients' families days before the 2013 NFL Draft. The purpose was to calm them down and reiterate that even in the worst case scenario, we had a great plan in place that would put their sons in a great position to make a club's 53-man roster the following September. As an undrafted rookie free agent, that is the most important factor when deciding which club to sign with following the NFL Draft. We were ready for the 2013 NFL Draft after four long months of preparation.

*   *   *   *

Draft Day(s) arrived. I use the term Day(s) in reference to the Thursday, Friday and Saturday reserved in late April or early May for all seven rounds of the NFL Draft. Day 1 covers the entire first round over a prolonged period of time. Day 2 wraps up the second and third rounds. Day 3 covers rounds four through seven, roughly 160 picks plus any Compensatory Draft Picks distributed under the CBA.[iv] My conversations with teams and the amount of pre-Draft activity suggested that Steven Means would be a late round pick and

Josh Kline had a chance to be drafted in the 7th round of the 2013 NFL Draft. Day 1 and Day 2 went by without either of my clients' names being called, something I fully expected.

Day 3 started off with a flurry of activity. The clubs that Steven and Josh worked out with during the pre-Draft process called and confirmed their health status and the level of interest they were garnering from other clubs. A significant amount of back and forth goes on in the mornings before the draft rounds kick off. The Tampa Bay Buccaneers came on late and expressed serious interest in Steven. They communicated this interest often. So did the Baltimore Ravens. I wasn't certain he would be drafted, but the number of draft picks Baltimore and Tampa had in the 5th, 6th and 7th rounds was a little reassuring.

Josh was generating serious interest from the Oakland Raiders and the Kansas City Chiefs. I spoke with both of them leading up to the start of Day 3. With 157 picks remaining in rounds four through seven, it was going to be an exciting day. I advised both of my clients to document who called them and when during the NFL Draft.

The time was 12:00 pm EST and Day 3 was underway. As the names came off the Draft board, I tracked every club's picks and revised my priority lists for Steven and Josh. In doing so, this would help my clients make the best decision if it were left up to them. I glanced up to see the Denver Broncos select Quanterus Smith with the 146th pick.

Tampa Bay was on the clock. Five minutes goes by pretty quickly in most situations. That is not the case when you are waiting for your client to be drafted. I looked at Steven's priority/interest list. While the interest was there, I wasn't certain the need was strong enough to use a 5th round pick for a defensive end, the position Steven was certain to play in Tampa. My phone rang. It was Steven.

Before I could decipher the words coming out of his mouth and the sheer jubilation in the background, Tampa's pick was submitted on the television. I knew what was coming next. "Steven Means" flashed across the screen for the entire world to see. The Tampa Bay

Buccaneers drafted Steven with the 147th pick in the 2013 NFL Draft.

I was elated. I told Steven to enjoy this moment. We would have work to do for Steven, but I had to shift my focus to Josh as the later rounds of the Draft approached. As teams drafted well into the 7th round, we both received calls from the five or six clubs that expressed interest in Josh. The tone of these calls suggested that he would go undrafted. One club we wanted to hear from but that hadn't contacted us yet was the New England Patriots. Half way through the 7th round, New England used its last pick on Steve Beauharnais, a linebacker from Rutgers.

Following the last pick of the Draft, the 32 NFL clubs are free to sign prospects that are not drafted in that year's Draft. The Patriots still had the fewest interior linemen under contract in the entire NFL. They did not draft an interior lineman to fulfill this need. I saw no reason for Josh to consider other clubs if, in fact, New England expressed interest in signing him. New England had a solid track record of retaining and developing undrafted players. I needed to determine if there were any interest on their end, so I reached out to my contact with the organization. We will call this person Joe.

I met Joe when I was a student in Ohio University's graduate program. I knew that my success as an agent would be tied to my connections with members of the NFL clubs, so I made certain to develop these relationships and maintain them going forward.

Joe picked up his cell phone on the third ring. I could hear the standard post-Draft hustle and bustle in the background, where teams have a limited window of time to sell themselves to the prospects that do not get drafted. This paradigm shift, where teams go from reluctant to communicate to eager to communicate, lasts for roughly 15-30 minutes or until the clubs get the prospects high on their preferred lists. It is bizarre, but it is part of the business.

Joe confirmed that New England was, in fact, interested in signing Josh Kline to an undrafted rookie deal. I told Joe that I would need to entertain the other clubs' offers, of which there were plenty, and speak with my client. I already knew my recommendation. Josh was excited about the potential to play at Gillette Stadium and agreed with my advice that New England presented the best opportunity to make the 53-man roster. I called Joe, used the interest from other clubs to secure a larger signing bonus and more guaranteed salary to protect Josh if he were waived, and agreed to terms with the New England Patriots.

My first NFL Draft as a sports agent was over, and I had two clients in the NFL. I looked at the ESPN scroll with Steven Means' name listed on the Draft results and began thinking about what it took to get to this point. As I watched the Draft recap, I received a text from a friend that worked at the NFL instructing me to look at the main TV above the NFL Draft stage at Radio City Music Hall. At the bottom of the screen in small font was my name with a personalized message congratulating me on my first NFL draft pick!

I was beyond excited. The dream I had since the age of 16 became a reality at 28 years of age. But I wasn't naïve. I knew the real work was just getting started. During voluntary workouts and training camp, I reached out to endorsers to establish a relationship and hopefully secure deals for Steven and Josh. A month later, I did my first merchandise endorsement deal with Nike. I communicated often with both clients, a quality I maintain to this day.

For Josh and Steven, a roster spot on the 53-man regular season roster wasn't a lock. Clubs in the NFL are permitted to carry 90 men on their rosters in the offseason. They are required to reduce this number two times during the preseason – once in the month of August and once in early September. The first trim down is to 75 men, and the last roster reduction occurs following the clubs' last preseason game. As of Saturday evening preceding the first Thursday night regular season game, teams are permitted to carry 53 men on their active/inactive rosters, excluding injured reserve players, practice squad players and other player designations outlined in the CBA. Since Steven was a fifth round pick and the Buccaneers had some money invested in him, he was a little more secure than Josh. This is why it was so important that we chose the best fit for Josh as an undrafted rookie. The odds of making the 53-man roster increase.

Early September arrived, and both players were informed that they had made their respective clubs' 53-man rosters. I was 28 years old in my first season as an NFL agent with two clients playing in the NFL.

*   *   *   *

I used this initial success to recruit heavily during the 2013 college football season. The following season(s) resulted in many disappointments similar to my recruiting efforts during the 2012 college football season, but I also added to my client list with a few prospects for the 2014 Draft that had a lot of potential. My client with the most potential was Jayrone Elliott, a defensive end from the University of Toledo that projected more as an outside linebacker in the NFL.

Jayrone didn't test exceptionally well, but I knew after watching him play and being reassured by his high school coach, Ted Ginn Sr., that Jayrone would make it at the next level. Jayrone visited with the Green Bay Packers as one of their Top 30 visits, and I was confident given their roster depth at outside linebacker and conversations with their scouting department that he would have a great shot at making the 53-man roster.

I advised Jayrone that his best chances of making it into the League if he went undrafted was with Green Bay. When Jayrone went undrafted, he received higher offers from the San Francisco 49ers and the New Orleans Saints, but I advised him that he should never compromise his best shot at making $420,000 on an active roster for a slightly higher signing bonus after the Draft (< $5,000 difference).

Jayrone took my advice, made the 53-man roster in Green Bay and led the Packers' special teams unit during the 2014 NFL season. Josh Kline started six contests for the Super Bowl Champion New England Patriots. Steven Means was released by the Buccaneers after week one and landed on his feet with the Baltimore Ravens as an outside linebacker.

The following year, I had six clients in the National Football League with three veterans and three rookies. I negotiated a two-year, $4.9 million extension for Josh Kline with the New England Patriots. Jayrone Elliott was named Sunday Night Player of the Week in Week 2 for his performance against the Seattle Seahawks. Steven Means was promoted to the Philadelphia Eagles' active roster.

My early success as an NFL agent increased the number of contacts I had across the Big Four. As I met these individuals serving in different roles and conducted business with them, I started to see that every position in sports is unique. I relied on feedback from these executives to advise students and young professionals that sought career advice from me following my time in the 49ers' front office and emergence as an NFL agent.

Part Two of this book identifies 11 different positions in the sports industry and offers career guidance from professionals currently occupying these roles. Understanding the various positions in the sports industry is the first step to crafting a successful networking plan.

As you read the narratives that follow in Part Two, I want you to remember that there is no universal blueprint for obtaining a certain position. Each position covered in this book presents its own challenges and obstacles. But you must understand the responsibilities, challenges and demands of a given occupation before you pursue that role with an organization. Part Two will equip you with this understanding and put you in a position to pursue and subsequently obtain the job of your dreams in sports, instead of becoming just another résumé in the trashcan. So let's get started.

PART TWO:
ANALYZING DIFFERENT ROLES IN THE SPORTS
INDUSTRY

3

GENERAL COUNSEL: THE EVOLVING ROLE OF ATTORNEYS IN SPORTS

Alec Scheiner – former Senior Vice President and General Counsel for the Dallas Cowboys and former President for the Cleveland Browns

"People who succeed in this business understand the importance of making other people's jobs easier."

Alec Scheiner served as General Counsel and Senior Vice President of the Dallas Cowboys from September of 2004 until December of 2012, when he joined the Cleveland Browns as President, a role he held until March of 2016. As President, he was responsible for overseeing the operations of the entire organization, including ticket sales, stadium operations, fan engagement, legal, finance, human resources, corporate partnerships and organizational strategy. I reconnected with Alec at the Browns' headquarters in Berea, Ohio, and witnessed the organizational transformation he led in Cleveland. Under his leadership, the Cleveland Browns went from 31st to 12th in overall profits and 26th to 19th in local revenues in a little over three years.

Alec's career in the sports industry didn't start as an unpaid intern or an entry-level employee. He didn't bounce around leagues and gain the practical experience that owners desire in the industry. He began as an attorney with a focus on international finance before transitioning into the sports industry. For him, his network played a more integral role in his development and transition into the sports industry than most executives.

His involvement in the business affairs of a professional sports franchise evolved over time, but never before had he steered the proverbial ship. As a leading sports executive capable of generating revenues and leading organizational transformations, Alec understands the NFL's and other professional sports leagues' business models and relies on this knowledge to outperform competitors, regardless of which organization he leads. Alec spent most of his time in the sports industry in a legal capacity, which is what he advises on in this chapter.

      *   *   *   *

Sport as a profession was not at the forefront of Alec's mind early in his life. He decided early in his adolescence that he wanted to be involved in foreign services, specifically, development in Latin America. Whether it was his father's influence during his time in Guatemala or his own immersion in their culture through various trips to this region, Alec was determined to make a difference in these areas. To that end, he enrolled at the School of Foreign Service at Georgetown University with a focus in Economics and Latin American development.

Although he had studied the culture and history of Latin America while enrolled at Georgetown, it wasn't until he worked for a non-profit in El Salvador that he developed an understanding of how business was conducted in Latin America. He played semi-pro basketball while working in El Salvador, but that was the extent of his involvement in sports. Professionally speaking, he realized he wouldn't be able to achieve what he had hoped to accomplish without a law degree. He decided to take the Law School Admission Test (LSAT).

Administratively speaking, taking the LSAT in the United States was and continues to be relatively simple. Things were a little bit different in El Salvador. For instance, the State of Ohio has 15 different testing centers that administer a total of 51 tests per year. In El Salvador, there were zero. In order to apply for law schools, Alec was informed that he would have to return to the States or Panama to take the LSAT. He petitioned the Law School Admission Council (LSAC) to administer the exam at the US Embassy in San Salvador, where he would be the only person taking the exam in 1993.

The LSAC approved. When his LSAT test results came back, his scores were high enough to apply for a foreign studies joint degree program at Georgetown Law and the Johns Hopkins School of Advanced International Studies. He was accepted into both schools but ultimately chose to pursue his juris doctorate at Georgetown Law.

Upon his graduation from Georgetown, Alec joined Wilmer Cutler Pickering Hale and Dorr, a prominent law firm currently known as WilmerHale. While he took the position with WilmerHale to continue working in Latin American Finance and Private Equity, he started to see a trend in the sports industry.

Advances in technology, privately financed stadiums, and forward-thinking ownership groups created demand for legal services and increased the popularity of professional sports around the world. Owners were acquiring assets, forming entities to manage the services offered at their venues, and securing capital to make that next big improvement. An attorney's role in the sports industry exceeded the everyday sponsorship agreement or human resources inquiry.

Dick Cass, a partner at the law firm, handled the majority of the firm's sports-related work. Alec expressed his interest in this type of work, and Dick agreed to loop him in when transactions came into the firm. His first exposure to transactional work in the sports industry came when another associate attorney at WilmerHale (Jay Bauman – now with the NFL) asked him if he wanted to assist with the due diligence review for Ted Leonsis' acquisition of the Washington Capitals and a share of the Washington Wizards. Alec jumped at the opportunity.

He continued his work in Latin American Finance. His relationship with Dick and Jay exposed him to other transactions in the sports industry through the firm's involvement in the financing and construction of sporting venues, which included the Rose Bowl stadium in Pasadena, CA, and the Baltimore Ravens' stadium in

Baltimore, MD. He also helped with the relocation of the Hornets to New Orleans and assisted with a minority ownership sale of the Toronto Raptors and Maple Leafs. Entering his sixth year at WilmerHale, the different sports projects he assisted with taught him that he wanted to make a career out of his work in the sports industry.

These different transactions also equipped Alec with the legal competencies that he would need to pursue a career as an attorney for a sports franchise. He performed due diligence reviews involved with the sale of a sports franchise (Washington Capitals and Wizards), executed a franchise relocation (Charlotte Hornets), secured professional sports leagues' approvals for partial sale of an organization (Toronto Raptors and Maple Leafs) and negotiated agreements for the financing of professional sports venues.

He worked diligently behind the scenes with Dick Cass on many transactions for Jerry Jones involving the Dallas Cowboys. This work continued until Dick informed him that he was considering leaving the firm to become President of the Baltimore Ravens. In Dick's absence, Alec wondered whether the firm could continue to maintain the level of sports-related work that he came to enjoy over the years.

He spoke with Dick, who offered to connect Alec and Jerry Jones to help further this relationship. His involvement in the legal issues on which WilmerHale provided counsel to the Jones family put him in a great position to continue serving the family, as well as other sports-related deals, subsequent to Dick's departure.

While reaching out to Jerry, Dick learned that he was weighing the option of hiring an in-house counsel to handle all legal matters for the organization. Most importantly, Jerry Jones was in the process of designing and building a new stadium in Arlington, Texas, and he needed someone that understood this process, as well as the NFL's CBA.

Owners who agreed to build new stadiums or undertake substantial renovations were permitted under the 2007 CBA to exclude certain revenues generated from these improvements from the calculation of Total Revenue, which determined the players' share of the profits.[v] In simpler terms, owners could use future profits to finance current improvements without having to worry about sharing those profits with the players. This in part led to the stadium boom in the early 21st century.

Jerry Jones had envisioned a new, state-of-the-art stadium for the Dallas Cowboys since the mid-to-late 1990's. In August of 2004, Arlington City Council agreed unanimously to put before voters a tax increase that would fund the city's $325 million portion of the construction of a new stadium for the Dallas Cowboys. This influx of cash to help finance the construction of the stadium, combined with the provision in the CBA that permitted owners to finance their improvements with future profits generated by these improvements, would help bring Jerry's vision to a reality. At the time of the proposed tax increase, all Jerry needed was an attorney familiar with the issues associated with constructing a new stadium and the NFL CBA. Alec understood both.

Thanks to his experience at WilmerHale, Alec had the perfect combination of experience and a strong understanding of what it would take to succeed as general counsel of a professional sports franchise.

He received word that the Dallas Cowboys were interested in interviewing him for the general counsel position. He flew to Irving, Texas, in August of 2004, without a clear understanding of who he would be meeting with and what they would discuss.

He had no idea what to expect, but he knew this would be a life changing opportunity. He prepared by performing extensive research, creating a PowerPoint presentation that highlighted what he could bring to the Dallas Cowboys and reiterating that it made economic sense to bring an attorney in-house. When he arrived for the interview, he was greeted by Jerry Jones, Stephen Jones and Jerry Jones Jr.

He was beyond surprised by the attendees. They asked him to describe his experience handling legal issues faced by team owners. His response to their question led to their realization that Alec handled the majority of the Cowboys' legal issues previously referred to outside counsel WilmerHale. This provided a level of comfort and familiarity with the family. He also displayed why he would be an asset to the Cowboys and how bringing him in-house would benefit the organization. He nailed the interview, and Dick Cass' glowing recommendation led to an offer.

Jerry was so persuasive that Alec ended up taking the job right then and there, before he even had a chance to talk it over with his wife. In September of 2004, he packed up his car and drove from New York City to Dallas as General Counsel for the Dallas Cowboys with his wife and golden retriever.

The tax increase was approved on November 2, 2004, and the stadium plans were underway. The construction of the stadium took precedence in the beginning. Alec was responsible for every legal/financial aspect of this project, including leasing agreements, financing documents, construction issues and miscellaneous projects necessary for the completion of the stadium. He is credited as one of the architects that put together the stadium's creative financing package.

The financing package was structured as a large loan with limited collateral and auction rate market, which at the time was very uncommon.[vi] The stadium project was financed during the financial market collapse, creating additional complexities and regulatory hurdles. When the financing was approved and the stadium was under construction, he participated in the bidding and contracting with non-Cowboy events that would be held at the stadium. He was involved in almost everything.

A project of this magnitude doesn't come without its fair share of hardships. For starters, problems arose when securing the land for the construction site via eminent domain. Also, keeping up with Jerry's vision of the stadium as "more than an NFL stadium" kept him busy. His contributions were instrumental to the development of the largest venue in the National Football League and one of the largest sports venues in the world.

Alec's role in the organization evolved after the construction of the stadium project was well underway. He was named Senior Vice President and General Counsel of the Dallas Cowboys in 2008. This title required additional tasks, such as the development of a football analytics system, human resources inquiries, budgeting and business planning. He was responsible for the contracts that determined how much head coach Wade Phillips, and subsequently head coach Jason Garrett, would get paid. He was involved in the formation of Legends Hospitality Management LLC, a concessions and hospitality company that would offer services at the Cowboys' stadium, as well as other professional venues.

Alec also focused on the efficiency of the organization and the overall employee satisfaction level. He was no longer just an attorney for the Dallas Cowboys. He slowly established himself as a trusted business advisor and valuable member of the organization.

He helped bridge the gap between the business office and football operations office, as a result of his involvement with personnel contracts and the development of a football analytics system. Generally speaking, the business/operations divide delineates responsibilities as on-the-field activities (scouting, salary cap, coaching, etc.) belonging to football operations and the off-the-field activities (sponsorships, marketing, sales, communications, etc.) housed on the business side. In-house legal departments typically lean significantly towards the business side. Alec's involvement in both earned him a seat in the Cowboys' personnel room where all the scouts and front office executives made decisions on Draft day.

His accomplishments while in Dallas netted him various awards acknowledging his business acumen and legal abilities. He was named to the *Sports Business Journal's* prestigious "40 Under 40" list in 2010. Alec served on the board of directors of Legends Hospitality, a concessionaire, sales and marketing company founded by the Dallas Cowboys and New York Yankees. Alec is also very involved with the MIT Sloan Sports Analytics Conference, which focuses on the increasing role of analytics in the global sports industry.

After spending eight years as in-house counsel and entering the last year of his employment contract with the Dallas Cowboys, Alec was ready to explore the business side of professional sports. He helped shape arguably one of the most historic franchises in professional sports. He was a driving force behind the stadium construction project and served as one of a few non-family members to the project. The exposure he received from the stadium project resulted in phone calls from organizations looking to add someone with Alec's knowledge of the stadium improvement process and ability to accomplish organizational realignment.

One such call came from Joe Banner towards the end of the 2012 NFL regular season. Alec paid close attention to how the division rival Philadelphia Eagles transformed the organization on both the football side and the business side under Joe's leadership. Joe was being considered for an executive role with a few different organizations in the NFL and NBA, and he informed Alec that he would like him to join him as President on his staff, wherever that may be.

He was ready for the challenge. His role with the Cowboys required more than just the day-to-day legal responsibilities, but his role as an attorney took precedence to his involvement on the business side. In this new role, he would be strictly business.

He waited patiently to see how things played out. But he set his priorities before he even knew if there would be a formal offer. He wanted to join an organization where a culture transformation was both necessary and possible. Pay wouldn't be the driving factor. The city wouldn't play a big part in his evaluation. The key was ownership's buy in to the idea of a culture shift. He eventually received offers. On December 18, 2012, Alec was named President of the Cleveland Browns.

*   *   *   *

Q & A: Alec Scheiner's Advice on Becoming General Counsel for a Professional Sports Franchise

Q. If you could offer some advice to individuals looking to break into the sports industry as an attorney, what would it be?

A. Positions in professional sports, whether with a league office or an organization, require a greater level of sophistication. The business has evolved and so have the professionals working in the industry, so you need a particular skill set just to get into the business. Once you get in with an organization using that skill set, then you can start to explore other responsibilities. For me, my skill set was the ability to negotiate, and then I could show my organizational and people skills.

Q. What is the best piece of professional advice you received during your career?

A. The best way to network is to do a great job.

Q. Who are the top five most influential people in your career, excluding family, and why?

A. (1) Dick Cass (President for the Baltimore Ravens) – He is living confirmation that you can be decent and strong with negotiations.

(2) Jerry Jones (Owner, President and General Manager for the Dallas Cowboys) – He always pushed me to think of the questions that no one else is asking. Stephen Jones (COO, EVP and Director of Player Personnel for the Dallas Cowboys) – He always stressed the importance of building and maintaining relationships with those you work with.

(3) Roberto Dañino (former Prime Minister of Peru) – He taught me the importance of caring for those who work for you.

(4) (a) Mike Rawlings (former CEO of Legends Hospitality, Mayor of Dallas) – He taught me that it is possible to combine terrific business acumen with true compassion for those who are less fortunate. (b) Dave Checketts (former CEO of Legends Hospitality and Founder of Checketts Fund) – He is a man of real grace and class who truly cares about people.

(5) Greg McElroy (former VP for the Cowboys, Associate AD for Arizona State) – He showed how important building relationships is and maintaining a work-life balance.

Q. When you look to hire someone, what is the most important quality or qualities you look for in an applicant?

A. A defined skill set and a strong recommendation.

Q. What advice do you offer to professionals aspiring to climb the corporate ladder in a professional sports league or within a particular sports franchise?

A. Dick Cass once told me that professional sports is not a difficult business. It is about people and processes. People who succeed in this business understand the importance of making other people's jobs easier and enhancing their perception of the value they bring to an organization.

Q. Any guidance with respect to how to secure a position in the sports industry?

A. Some news that was passed along to me and held true over time is that you have to be willing to relocate and move anywhere. If you are willing to move anywhere, be certain to do great work when the opportunity presents itself.

Q. What advice can you give attorneys looking to break into sports with the intention of becoming president of an organization?

A. State your desire to learn as much about the organization and the business as you can, and when an opportunity presents itself, don't be afraid to take on responsibilities in an area outside of your comfort zone.

Q. What is your most memorable moment as an employee in the industry?

A. When Dallas beat the Philadelphia Eagles in the 2009 Playoffs. We went 3-0 against Philly that season.

*   *   *   *

"Ask the questions that no one else is asking." Alec acknowledged that Jerry Jones has been very influential in his career because he challenged him to do this during his time in Dallas. His career path suggests that he was asking the questions that no one else was asking long before he arrived in Dallas. He did this when he petitioned the LSAC and requested authorization to take the LSAT at the U.S. Embassy in San Salvador. He did this to gain exposure at WilmerHale and secure sports-related work. Perhaps Jerry Jones didn't teach Alec to think this way but instead he placed him in an environment that would allow him to continue thinking in this manner.

While this way of thinking is important, it wasn't Alec's ticket into professional sports. Alec's story is different than any other career path highlighted in this book, in that he decided later in his life that he wanted to work in sports.

For individuals looking to break into the sports industry later in their professional careers, the key takeaway is that you need a strong enough network and well-connected mentors that will put their necks on the line and recommend you for a position. Owners of professional sports franchises want to see experienced applicants when a position in their organization is vacant. This is especially true for positions of significant importance, such as legal counsel. These relationships are fundamental in order to convince ownership that a particular applicant can handle the responsibilities of the job.

Individuals working outside the sports industry should connect with as many professionals that occupy their desired role as possible. Use these relationships to understand the demands of the position, the desired skill sets, and the variables that determine success v.

failure. When working outside of sports, you need to align yourself with individuals that can influence decision makers. Building this strong of a relationship takes time, but it is necessary to make a lateral move into an executive level position.

For individuals that desire to work in sports as an attorney, specifically as an in-house counsel in the Big Four, Alec's path represents the traditional approach. This approach should not be relied upon. The time to look for opportunities with sports organizations is while you are a law student; in the form of unpaid internships and volunteer opportunities. Upon graduation, loans enter repayment, additional loans are no longer available and the demands of everyday life make it very difficult to work for free or for limited wages as a licensed attorney.

It is also important to understand how saturated this aspect of the sports industry has become. The American Bar Association reported that in 2015, there were 1,300,705 licensed attorneys in the United States. [vii] There are 122 sports teams in the Big Four. Assuming every club has only one attorney on staff, options are incredibly limited. I understand not every attorney wants to work in sports, but after passing the bar exam and searching for employment in a legal capacity with a sports team, I can tell you first-hand that it is incredibly competitive.

Legal internships and volunteer positions in sports provide an opportunity to build a stronger network of legal professionals working in sports and to identify the different areas of law that attorneys need to understand in order to counsel professional sports organizations effectively. These experiences will shape your curriculum in the remaining years of law school and influence which direction you go post-law school.

Securing a position with a large law firm with a substantial sports practice is the ideal next step following the bar exam. As Alec's story suggests, these opportunities are very limited and require a combination of legal competence and fortuitous circumstances. If an opportunity with one of these firms does not exist, identify opportunities that will develop your understanding of the law in the different areas that impact sports organizations.

Alec used a combination of creative thinking, business acumen, and interpersonal skills to step outside his comfort zone and climb the executive ladder in professional sports. His unique skill sets and ability to execute on a vision make him a valuable asset to almost any sports team. But more important than all these positive qualities, he never stopped "asking the questions that no one else is asking." Alec will continue to ask these questions and come up with the solutions. He encourages others to do the same.

4

CHIEF OPERATING OFFICER: GENERATING REVENUE AND BEYOND

Andy Dolich – former Chief Operating Officer for the San Francisco 49ers

"Manage your career/life through the windshield, not the rear view mirror."

Andy Dolich's career as a sports business executive has spanned over 40 years and includes positions as Administrative Assistant, Director of Marketing, Executive Vice President of Business Operations, President, President of Business Operations and Chief Operating Officer (COO) with the Philadelphia 76ers, Washington Capitals, Oakland Athletics, Golden State Warriors, Vancouver/Memphis Grizzlies and the San Francisco 49ers, respectively. He has held an executive position in each of the Big Four professional sports leagues.

My first interaction with him occurred when I was in graduate school. Andy, who at the time was COO for the San Francisco 49ers, led a webinar focused on launching a career in the sports industry. Throughout his career, his focus and passion was revenue generation. Andy was COO for the 49ers from December of 2007 until April of 2010. He was responsible for revenue growth and running every business-related activity for the organization. Through this experience and many others, he offers a unique perspective on what it takes to become Chief Operating Officer for a professional sports franchise.

*   *   *   *

Andy was 11 years old when he enrolled in Sports Appreciation, an after-school enrichment program offered at his elementary school. While he didn't dream about a career in sports at the time, this class helped him identify one of his passions at a young age.

His interest in sports eventually became more than recreational. He attended American University, where he focused on government and international politics. He grappled for ways to keep his love of sports alive. His answer was becoming a walk-on, non-scholarship basketball player. This lasted for two seasons, when he hung up the sneakers to pursue practical experiences in sports.

As a junior, he was named Student Director of Intramural Sports and worked with the Sports Information Director (SID), Mike Trilling, at American University. These experiences solidified Andy's desire to work in sports. He spent the remainder of his time at American University figuring out how to position himself for a career in sports.

Andy graduated in 1969 and planned on immediately pursuing his master's degree, but, shortly after his graduation, his father suffered a serious heart attack. Putting his family first, he delayed graduate school to stay home with his parents while his father recovered. He learned about Ohio University's Masters of Sports Administration, which was the first program of its kind in the United States. He focused on this possibility and submitted his application. He was accepted into Ohio University's graduate program in 1970.

He relocated to Athens, Ohio, in pursuit of his master's degree. He settled in for the first few weeks, after which he began networking. Andy sent letters to various professionals working in the sports industry. One particular letter that was responded to came from Ron Bain, former Executive Vice President at CBS Sports. Ron told him to come to the Blackrock building in New York and he would meet with him, which Andy did.

The program at Ohio University was under the direction of Dr. James Mason. As opportunities surfaced, he would review the opportunities and do his best to pair students whose interests aligned with the opportunities presented. He informed Andy about an internship opportunity with the Philadelphia 76ers.

The 76ers' general manager was Don DeJardin, a leading executive with a military background who appreciated hard work. He set aside up to four internships for Ohio University students and indicated that he would hire the student that accomplished success in the tasks they were given. Andy Dolich was selected as one of the three interns in 1971.

He performed general tasks as assigned. He sold souvenirs. He helped facilitate fan giveaways for the 76ers, statistically the worst team in the NBA. Andy also played the role of Uber driver before the days of Uber and minus the ride fee. One recipient of his "taxi service" was Red Auerbach, the legendary head coach of the Boston Celtics. He often reflects on that car ride, which taught him to be willing to put himself out there and do the small jobs that can become the big breaks. While the conversations were kept to a minimum, Coach Auerbach encouraged Andy to "do whatever it takes and one day, it might result in you becoming President of a professional sports team."

After his internship, he was hired full time by the 76ers as an Administrative Assistant to the General Manager. This opportunity allowed him to see the sports industry through a much larger lens, and his involvement assisting the general manager of an NBA franchise allowed him to catch a glimpse of what it takes to run an organization. Over time, his focus with the organization shifted to ticket sales.

Selling tickets was a different world back in 1971. There were no secondary markets, electronic tickets, prospecting services, sales analytics/metrics or online selling tools. Andy was handed a map of downtown Philadelphia and South Jersey and went door-to-door, business-to-business with one goal in mind...to sell season tickets. He didn't have a sales quota, but he did everything he could to make a sale. He continued to sell tickets in this role for three years when he learned about an opportunity with the National Lacrosse League.

The start-up National Lacrosse League had a successful team in Philadelphia. One of the owners was considering an expansion team in Washington and was looking for someone to run their business operations. While this league was viewed as an outlier to the Big Four, he perceived this career opportunity as one step back and two steps forward in his career.

"I would analyze every opportunity on a legal pad divided into halves," Andy explained. "On one side, I would list the positives of my current position, and I would do the same on the other side for the new role. If the new job provided more positives than negatives and offered a new skill set, I leaned towards the new position regardless of the sports league."

Based on this analysis, he included his name in the search and was eventually hired as Vice President of Business Operations for the Maryland Arrows. The Arrows were a lesser-known team in a smaller market, but Andy understood that this position would give him a leg up on the marketing side of the business, which might help him secure a similar position in the Big Four. He relied on this approach to land subsequent roles as Director of Marketing for the Washington Capitals and Executive Vice President and General Manager for the Washington Diplomats of the North American Soccer League (NASL).

In these roles, he focused on everything from marketing, promotions, advertising, customer service and leadership training to sales responsibilities. As General Manager for the Washington Diplomats, he built strong relationships with youth soccer organizations, which ultimately led to increased attendance and sales. Andy identified this untapped segment of the market and went after it. His experiences in these roles and the skills sets he acquired positioned him well when he received a phone call from Matt Levine regarding a position with the Oakland Athletics.

Matt was the founder of Pacific Select, a sports business consulting firm, and the author of the first published newsletter distributed to sports professionals that is now viewed as the precursor to the Sports Business Journal. Andy initially connected with Matt when he was working for the 76ers and Matt was doing consulting work for the NBA and NHL. They would cross paths periodically at different league meetings, but it wasn't until the Haas family acquired the Oakland Athletics from Charlie Finley and hired Matt to assemble a front office staff that their relationship would elevate both of their careers.

Matt reached out to Andy and asked him if he would be interested in interviewing for Vice President of Business Operations for the Oakland Athletics. He jumped at the opportunity.

He was one of many interviewees that underwent a rigorous interview process. He made it to the final interview with the Haas family, when Mr. Haas asked him, "You've been in sports awhile now. What can you tell us about our investment here in professional baseball?" Andy responded, "The quickest way to become a millionaire as the owner of a professional sports team is to start out as a multi-millionaire."

Roy Eisenhardt, then-President for the Oakland Athletics, offered him the position, which he turned down.

Andy was married with a one-year-old son when the job was offered. The timing was difficult, and they believed that it was best for the family to get a little more established before uprooting and moving across the country. He found himself thinking a lot about the position after he turned it down.

The more he thought about it, the more he convinced himself that this was his golden opportunity. He was a believer in the "seek out chaos and disaster" approach for professional success, which the circumstances in Oakland presented at the time that the position was offered. According to Andy, "If you can learn to sell and generate revenue in dismal situations, opportunities will surface and elevate your career."

He called Roy Eisenhardt the following week and asked if the position was still available. He replied, "If you are willing to say yes and accept on this call, then the job is yours." Andy was hired by the Haas family as Vice President of Business Operations for the Oakland Athletics in November of 1980.

The A's finished 12th overall in the 1980 season with a record of 83 wins and 79 losses. Despite this finish, the Athletics' average attendance during the 1980 season was 10,398. This ranked them 24 out of the 26 clubs in Major League Baseball.[viii]

His first task was to assemble a sales staff that would increase season ticket sales and promote the brand. Four employees handled the Athletics' business operations when he arrived. His first two hires were proven leaders and professionals on the business side. Together, they built a sales staff with 32 employees in only 45 days. The Athletics had an MLB-low 326 season ticket holders at the end of the 1980 season. By the start of the 1981 season, they had sold 3,500 season tickets. The Athletics' average attendance increased from 10,398 per game in 1980 to roughly 24,000 in 1981.[ix]

The success didn't stop in 1981 and it wasn't isolated to the business offices. The team played well, winning 11 games straight and 16 out of 17 to start the 1981 season. Andy and his team of business operations marketers focused on driving attendance by making a night at the ballpark the most affordable and entertaining experience for families in the community. He looked at the fan experience and installed activities like the Speed Pitch (fans could throw at a radar gun to determine pitch speed) and on-field activities that increased fan engagement.

The organization continued to build momentum, which led to the A's hosting the 1987 All-Star Game in front of 16,500 season ticket holders. Three consecutive World Series trips in 1988-1990, resulting in one World Championship, furthered the organization's success. But this momentum wouldn't last forever.

He saw changes in the organization, including the Haas family's decision to shuffle the control of management, which led him to consider opportunities as they presented themselves. There was an opportunity next door with the Golden State Warriors.

Chris Cohan purchased the Warriors and looked to bring in his own staff. Tod Leiweke, who served as President for the Warriors and was preparing for his departure from the organization, recommended Andy as his successor. Andy interviewed and was named President for the Golden State Warriors.

On the spectrum of professional experiences, his stint with the Warriors was on the opposite end from his experience with the Haas family in Oakland. Andy's vision didn't align with Chris Cohan's demands, and he found himself on his way out of the Warriors' organization less than a year after leaving the Oakland Athletics. He used his contract buyout money to form his own consulting business and test the waters of self-employment. According to him, "Working in sports requires you to move around, and if you can pay the bills on your own, it empowers you to take risks with the comfort that you can make it work if an opportunity doesn't pan out."

On his way back into the Big Four, Andy worked for a start-up company that is now Tickets.com. He continued to generate revenue at every level, and his ability to do so attracted the Vancouver Grizzlies. He received a strong recommendation from the Chicago Bulls' Executive Vice President, which was also shared with Michael Heisley, the then-owner of the Grizzlies. Shortly thereafter, Andy was named President of Business Operations for the Vancouver Grizzlies.

He went on to serve in this role for eight years (one in Vancouver and seven in Memphis after the team relocated) and led everything from revenue generation to strategic planning for the construction of FedEx Forum, the Grizzlies' new arena that opened in 2004. He and his team were responsible for the construction of the Forum and the Grizzlies' business operations.

In 2007, the San Francisco 49ers initiated a search to fill their vacant Chief Operating Officer role. They were searching for an executive with proven revenue generation abilities, which Andy demonstrated by securing a $100 million naming rights deal with FedEx for the Grizzlies' arena and leading other revenue generating activities for organizations across the Big Four.

Team owner John York hired Andy as Chief Operating Officer for the San Francisco 49ers in December of 2007. He was hired to accomplish three major objectives: (1) lead the stadium construction efforts from a revenue generation standpoint (personal seat licenses, seat revenue, presentation of sponsorships, etc.), (2) develop the sales infrastructure to meet ownership's demands, and (3) manage the existing business units to drive revenue, including corporate sponsorships, ticket sales, marketing, partnerships and all activities related to the business side.

He prioritized internalizing the 49ers' ticket sales operations. In his opinion, the more people selling who were directly affiliated with the organization, the more tickets sold. His other focus was sponsorships. He wanted to use the leverage of a new stadium to tap some of the corporate resources in the Silicon Valley and surrounding areas. Andy's goal was to increase ticket sales and sponsorship activity in anticipation of the new stadium.

While progress was made on the business side, the team failed to perform on the field, and changes were made across the board. From an ownership perspective, John York handed over his responsibilities to his son, Jed. Within one year of this transition, he sensed that his time was coming to an end. Andy was let go in March of 2010.

His departure marked the last time he would work directly for a professional sports franchise. He reopened his consulting business and now serves as Managing Director and Head of the U.S. Sports Practice at Odgers and Berndtson, an international executive search firm based in London. He also serves as an advisor to various companies operating in different segments of the industry, including The Basketball Tournament (TBT), Accelerate Sports, Navigate Marketing, Playyon, Project Fanchise and Vhere.

Based on his 40+ years of experience in the sports industry, Andy relies on his knowledge to write weekly columns for csnbayarea.com. He explores everything from stadium construction to futuristic revenue streams. He also inspires young professionals by teaching courses at Stanford University and serving as the Director of Career Development at the University of San Francisco's master's program in collegiate athletics. He is still driven to learn, and with the desire to learn, comes the ability to teach. For aspiring COOs, Andy's career path and the resulting advice will help one navigate the business side of professional sports and secure a position as COO.

*   *   *   *

Q & A: Andy Dolich's Advice on Succeeding as Chief Operating Officer for a Professional Sports Franchise

Q. Where do you see the industry going in the next 5 years? 10 years?

A. It will incorporate sponsorship company names as part of the teams – this is already being done in the WNBA, Barclays Premier League and NFL training camp uniforms. Virtual reality will become a part of teams' broadcasts and websites.

Q. How has the industry changed since you started in the business?

A. It is too difficult to summarize these changes in a few sentences. A few themes that highlight the changes in the industry include (1) relationships have become more important because the industry is more competitive, (2) very little loyalty across the board, and (3) emerging professionals with all the intelligence, but limited experience and understanding of the industry.

Q. Name one person that helped you break into the industry?

A. The late Mike Trilling.

Q. Your best piece of networking advice?

A. Quadruple the number of people you have in your "A Network."

Q. Who are the top 5 most influential people in your career/network?

A. (1) My wife and three children.

(2) Matt Levine (Sports Business Consultant) – His advice and general philosophies that you didn't have to be with a winning team or super star team to be successful.

(3) Mike Trilling (Sports Information Director for American University) – "Trills" was a single guy that was 24/7 sports without playing a damn thing in his life. This showed me a side of sports that I never would have seen and led me to read about OU.

(4) Pat Williams (former General Manager for the Orlando Magic) – He came to the 76ers after I left the organization, and he brought showmanship to the game (ultimate promoter) and did a lot of crazy things, out of the box ideas to promote the sport. He channeled Bill Veeck. He always has time for people and is an exceptional public speaker – a great communicator.

(5) Wally Haas & Roy Eisenhardt (Owner and President for the Oakland Athletics, respectively) – Wally, who was Walter Haas Sr.'s son, and Roy were in charge of the organization and Walter was a hands-off owner. They taught me that sports could be used to give back to the community.

Q. What advice do you have for someone looking to enter a different area of an organization from his/her current position?

A. Find an executive in the organization who will listen, tell you the truth and help guide you.

Q. What would you tell aspiring COO's at the beginning of their career?

A. Seek out "chaos and disaster." Find an environment where you can make intelligent mistakes and not lose your job. Also, keep your career close and your family closer.

Q. Given your experiences with different organizations in various professional leagues, what advice do you have for professionals considering a jump to another organization?

A. My experiences are limited to professional sports, so I would view teams as a pyramid, with ownership at the top. The real successful franchises have a well-balanced organization, and the ones that are imbalanced will ultimately fail.

Q. What advice do you have for someone looking to secure a position on the business side of professional sports?

A. Opportunities on the business side are greater in number, so you have a better chance of getting a job on the business side than the team operations side. Hone your sales skills every day in every way.

Q. What is your most memorable moment in the sports industry?

A. No one moment. It is the thousands of moments walking around venues seeing people from every possible background, age, demographic, level of interest having a great time with smiles on their faces watching great athletes in an unscripted setting.

Q. What is the one thing that every employer looks for in hiring an employee?

A. A well-rounded personality is key for me. I want diplomatic contrarians who define themselves by who they are not what they do.

*   *   *   *

I first met Andy in person at a coffee shop in Santa Clara, CA, two miles from Levi's Stadium, the new home of the San Francisco 49ers. We represented polar opposites. He had 40+ years of experience working in professional sports and the stories to show for it. I was starting my first month in the sports industry and was as naive as they came. Fast forward five years. The advice he provided to me at that coffee shop is displayed throughout this chapter and in his responses above.

Andy encourages aspiring COOs to set aside public perceptions to identify opportunities with responsibilities that will equip you with the skills necessary to become a COO. He shared his process when evaluating a job offer or vacant position in the area of his interest. While his process wasn't particularly earth shattering, it raises a good point: You should evaluate a position and identify whether it will provide/enhance a skill set necessary for a particular role.

He wanted to be in charge of all business operations for a professional sports team. He made a conscious decision to leave positions with organizations in the Big Four in pursuit of positions in smaller sports leagues that would equip him with a required skill set. His decisions didn't come without risk, and his time with the Golden State Warriors serves as a reminder of this.

He also encourages aspiring COOs and sports professionals to "quadruple the number of people you have in your 'A Network,' which I have defined as *the group of professionals that truly understand the market/position of your interest and can have an influence on your career in sports.* Connecting with these individuals increases the odds of obtaining a desired role in the industry.

How to connect with these potential "A Network" professionals is up to you. Connecting at the level Andy suggests takes more than emails and sporadic conversations. It requires creativity. Always be thinking of ways to connect. And most importantly, always be thinking of ways to convince them to help you as part of your "A Network."

He has been all over the sports industry. He's worked for ownership groups ranging from exceptional pioneers in the industry to complete duds. He's been hired. He's been fired. He has worked for himself. And he has relocated numerous times. These experiences taught him what it would take to lead the entire business operations of a professional sports organization as COO.

Learning the intricacies of the sports business takes time and requires different experiences. Andy obtained his level of knowledge over the course of 40+ years with eight organizations. He encourages others to identify similar opportunities and rely on the help of their "A Network" to ultimately land the opportunities that will position them to become COO of a sports franchise.

5

ASSISTANT GENERAL MANAGER: ONWARD AND UPWARD

Kevin Abrams – Assistant General Manager for the New York Giants

"Know exactly what is expected of you and how to identify the best way to get it accomplished."

Two continents, three different sports leagues, six part-time positions, and very supportive family and friends. That's what it took for Kevin Abrams to become the Assistant General Manager of the New York Giants. But as he stood on the turf in Glendale, Arizona, after Super Bowl XLII while confetti fell on the World Champion New York Giants, it was all worth it. His career path through the industry included stints in corporate relations, public relations, training camp operations, player personnel and salary cap management.

It took him eight years to go from a college graduate with a passion for sports business to an Assistant General Manager in the NFL. I couldn't help but ask myself, "What is it about Kevin Abrams that has allowed him to experience so much success in the New York Giants' organization?"

I met Kevin for dinner in late June, which is considered the vacation period for those in the NFL who work in football operations. Free agency is in the books and the draft has come and gone. This period from late June until training camp in late July provides a nice break from the excessive hours worked during the NFL season and free agency period. With every one of the Giants' players under contract, this was a perfect time to capture his path into the industry. I learned very quickly why Kevin ascended to become a key player in the New York Giants' front office before his 31st birthday.

*   *   *   *

Growing up in Ontario, Kevin viewed sports as more of a form of entertainment and enjoyment through participation rather than as a profession. Upon graduation from college, he considered law school as a viable option, and he took a job with a jewelry manufacturing company to begin saving for his journey to become a lawyer.

Kevin also volunteered as a football coach while working in Ontario. This was something he always wanted to do after graduating college. Everything was in place. He was working and saving money in preparation for three years of law school. But he felt something wasn't right. Despite everything coming together for the next step in his professional career, Kevin did a 180 and began to question his future in the legal profession. If he were going to go down this path, he wanted to make sure it was truly his passion. He set up a lunch meeting with a family friend Howie Starkman, the Public Relations Director for the Toronto Blue Jays, to learn more about the sports industry.

Howie informed him that the lack of an illuminated career path into the sports industry makes it difficult to provide advice to a young, aspiring student. But he advised Kevin that if he wanted to break into sports, he would need to quit his job, continue coaching, apply to Ohio University's graduate sports management program and gain practical experience in the industry. This conversation had a profound impact on Kevin's career path, and ultimately, on the advice he gives to young professionals.

Shortly thereafter, he decided against law school and shifted his professional focus to the sports industry. It was a tough decision for him to risk foregoing the financial security and clear career path that law school would have offered, but he was determined to make it in the sports industry. He left his job with the jewelry manufacturing company for an unpaid internship with Football Ontario, a move he viewed as a necessary step for gaining admission into Ohio University's graduate sports program.

Football Ontario served as the governing body for amateur and youth league football in Ontario. The organization supported youth leagues through fundraising initiatives, hosted coaching clinics, certified coaches across the province and implemented programs to improve participation. This was Kevin's first non-coaching position in the sports industry. It provided him with the practical experience that he lacked to be considered as an applicant for a graduate program focused on sports business.

After his internship concluded, he pursued Howie's second piece of advice, which was to obtain his master's degree in sports administration at a school with a great alumni network. This advice led him to apply to Ohio University, which was regarded as the top master's program with a concentration in sports. Ohio University's admissions process was extremely selective and targeted applicants with previous experience in the industry, which, thanks to Football Ontario, Kevin had. He was accepted into the program in September of 1996 and moved to Athens, Ohio, to begin his studies.

He settled into the program and remained mindful of Howie's advice that practical experience is of the utmost importance. Immediately upon arriving at school, he pursued and secured a volunteer position with the football staff assisting with recruiting. Then, two-thirds of the way to completing his master's program, he was made aware of an available internship with the London Monarchs.

The London Monarchs, a professional American football team in NFL Europe, served primarily as a development league for NFL clubs. As such, the players and coaches were primarily from the United States. An alumnus of Ohio University who worked in Corporate Relations for the London Monarchs knew that Ohio had a great sports program, so he reached out to the Executive Director of the program, Dr. Andrew Kreutzer, in search of an ideal candidate for a corporate relations intern. Dr. Kreutzer knew that Kevin wasn't sold on this aspect of professional sports, but he also knew that he wanted to work in the NFL.

The individuals Kevin spoke with when considering his career change reiterated that he needed to obtain a position with an NFL property to get the NFL shield on his résumé. Working for an organization in NFL Europe satisfied this objective. Despite being 3,950 miles from Athens, Ohio, and in a department outside his long-term interest of working in scouting and football operations, Kevin received Dr. Kreutzer's recommendation. He went through the interview process and subsequently received an offer to join the Monarchs.

Kevin had a great-aunt living in London who offered her guestroom free of charge for the duration of his internship, which made it financially possible for him to accept the internship. He moved to London, where he would be responsible for fulfilling sponsorships, running game day events, and coordinating grass roots marketing initiatives.

The internship lasted roughly four months. This experience taught him that sometimes working in a smaller organization (compared to an NFL franchise) provides an intern with a more valuable experience due to greater responsibilities. While his tenure with the Monarchs confirmed that his passion wasn't corporate relations, his time in London enabled him to put the NFL shield on his résumé.

Prior to moving to London, Kevin spoke with an alumnus of Ohio's program, Scott Berchtold, regarding the potential for a future opportunity in the Buffalo Bills' Public Relations department. He took the initiative and paid for a plane ticket so that he could interview in person for this opportunity. During his interview, it was discovered that the timing between the termination of the London Monarchs internship and the beginning of this position with the Bills aligned perfectly. He would be able to finish his internship with the Monarchs before the internship with Buffalo would be made available. The interview went well, and before Kevin headed off to London to join the Monarchs, he was offered the internship with the Bills upon his return.

It just so happened that he had family friends who lived in Buffalo, and, just as his great-aunt had done in London, they offered him a place to stay for the duration of his internship with the Bills. He is the first to admit that he was rather fortuitous with respect to the support system he had in place in the cities where these opportunities presented themselves.

In Buffalo, Kevin was responsible for everything ranging from proofing press releases to drafting game notes. He facilitated player interviews, which occurred on a frequent basis when the locker room was not open to the public. He would gather the equipment and make sure reporters and media sources were aware of the availability of the players. Lastly, he would help manage the press box on game days. His tenure in Buffalo lasted seven months and concluded with the last regular season game of the NFL season.

Kevin returned to campus and continued to look for opportunities to gain practical experience. He worked special events like the NBA All-Star Game, the Cotton Bowl and the Baseball Winter Meetings. While working these events, his responsibilities included fan relations, VIP services and event operations. While his primary interest was professional football, he worked these events to gain an understanding of an area completely unfamiliar to him that would help him connect with individuals working in sports.

When Kevin completed his degree, his experience included assisting the football coaching staff at Ohio University with their recruiting efforts; volunteering at the Cotton Bowl, the NBA All-Star Game and the Baseball Winter Meetings; and interning with the London Monarchs and Buffalo Bills. He had the NFL Shield on his résumé, experience in recruiting, player evaluation, event operations, corporate relations, marketing and public relations, as well as an expanded network in professional sports. He received his degree from Ohio University and was issued a one-year visa to work in his field of study. He was ready for his next opportunity.

Many teams in the NFL offer training camp internships that typically last four-to-six weeks. These opportunities provide a great way for people to break into the business and build a stronger network. He was notified of one such opportunity with the Washington Redskins through a connection he had made while working for the London Monarchs. His co-worker in London had previously interned with the Washington Redskins, and he offered to make a strong recommendation for Kevin. This recommendation led to a phone interview, and Kevin was subsequently offered a training camp internship with the Redskins.

He accepted this position heading into the 1998 season. The internship in Washington provided Kevin with his first opportunity to work in an NFL personnel department. His responsibilities included putting together tape cut ups, preparing scouting materials for the pro and college scouts, and assisting with training camp operations. Most importantly, he had the opportunity to work for general manager Charley Casserly. Charley joined the Washington Redskins in 1977 as an unpaid intern, and since that time, went on to win three Super Bowls during his 23-year tenure. But more importantly and directly linked with Kevin's career path, Charley Casserly reinstituted the Redskins' internship program in 1983.

As a product of the internship program himself, Charley and the rest of the staff in Washington respected hard work and dedication, two characteristics that defined Kevin's path through the sports industry. This experience allowed him to add to his network a highly reputable league executive that was willing to advocate for him and attest to his competencies in a professional setting. He spent his time in Washington learning about scouting and football operations.

As his term was set to expire with the Redskins, Kevin answered the office phone, a task ancillary to his specific responsibilities with the organization. The voice on the other end was Trip MacCracken, a former intern under Charley Casserly and current intern at the NFL Management Council. Over the course of the conversation, they discussed their respective careers and goals. Trip mentioned that he was returning to Duke for law school at the same time that Kevin's internship with the Redskins concluded. He also informed Kevin that the Management Council internship was still vacant for the upcoming regular season and recommended that he apply.

He interviewed with the Management Council and was offered the internship. He moved to New York with the intention of learning about an entirely new area of professional football: the salary cap.

The NFL implemented the salary cap in 1993 to combat escalating player salaries and widening revenue gaps between the small market clubs and the large market clubs. He didn't suspect that the salary cap would be his golden ticket into the NFL on a full-time basis; however, he did understand that this position would allow him to expand his knowledge of the NFL's business model and an important part of football operations that he had had no previous experience with. After Kevin accepted this opportunity with the Management Council, his professional résumé looked something like this:

     [✓] Communications (Buffalo Bills)
     [✓] Corporate Relations (London Monarchs)
     [✓] Coaching (Football Ontario)
     [✓] Player Personnel (Washington Redskins)
     [✓] Salary Cap & Contracts (Management Council)

This position allowed him to develop an additional skill set that would be valuable to any of the 32 organizations, and after nine months with the Management Council, he had a working knowledge of the salary cap, the player personnel rules, and the NFL's Collective Bargaining Agreement. Around that time in the mid-to-late 1990's, clubs realized the importance of addressing the need for an analyst to control the club's annual salary cap and cash positions.

The New York Giants contacted the Management Council in 1999 to find someone to manage their salary cap. Even though Kevin was semi-new to the Management Council, his name was included in the applicant pool. The Giants received strong recommendations on his behalf from Peter Ruocco (NFL Management Council) and Charley Casserly (Washington Redskins). He interviewed and had the experience to talk about during his interviews. The interviews went well, and he was offered his first full-time position in professional sports in the summer of 1999. He gladly accepted and was named Salary Cap Analyst for the New York Giants.

For the first time in his career in professional sports, Kevin accepted an offer without giving thought to which relative's guestroom he could occupy. He had made it as a full-time employee in the sports industry, and equipped with the knowledge that he had retained during his journey, he had every intention of remaining there for a long time.

Initially he was responsible for developing a system to manage the team's cap and cash positions. This presented enough challenges to justify a full-time position in the first year. However, Kevin had the foresight to perform tasks outside his role as a salary cap manager while hopefully enhancing his value to the organization. It was then that his experience with three different teams in three different departments came in handy.

He educated the scouts in the Giants' personnel department about player contracts and the Collective Bargaining Agreement. In return, the Giants' personnel directors educated him on college and pro scouting. He has been evaluating players ever since. The New York Giants rewarded his hard work by promoting him to Assistant General Manager in 2002.

In his current role, Kevin is responsible for assisting with the salary cap, negotiating player contracts, strategic planning for football operations, football technology and sports sciences initiatives and evaluating pro and college prospects. He also serves as the Giants' liaison with the League office in New York City. He established a strong relationship with Ernie Accorsi, who would go on to be one of Kevin's greatest mentors in the industry.

He has experienced two Super Bowl championships as Assistant General Manager of the New York Giants. He navigated the murky waters of the salary cap and established a process that would allow the New York Giants to maintain a healthy cap position. He maintained the principles instilled in him by mentors like Ernie Accorsi, Jerry Reese and Charley Casserly, and he used their advice to make a difference in the sports industry and the surrounding community alike. Kevin reflected on his experiences in the sports industry, acknowledging his good fortunes in sports "working for the best sports organization in the best city in the world." His sense of humility has remained intact, despite his level of professional success.

Kevin has been involved in many charitable efforts since his promotion to Assistant General Manager of the New York Giants in 2002. These efforts include sitting on Ohio University's Sports Administration Advisory Board, contributing significantly to the Cystic Fibrosis Foundation and supporting the You Can Play project, which promotes safety and inclusion in sport for LGBTQ athletes. Regardless of the cause, he strives to use the power of sport to benefit society as a whole.

In a little over 14 years, he learned the ins and outs of the operations side of sports business and went from working for a jewelry manufacturer to owning arguably the most highly coveted piece of jewelry as an Assistant General Manager in the NFL.

*   *   *   *

Q & A: Kevin Abrams' Advice on Becoming an Assistant General Manager in the National Football League

Q. If you could offer some advice to individuals looking to break into the sports industry, what would it be?

A. *Know exactly what is expected of you and how to identify the best way to get it accomplished. Always be developing your skill set so that you bring more value to an organization, while creating opportunities for yourself.*

Q. What is the best piece of professional advice you received during your career?

A. *Early in your career, don't make career choices based on money. Evaluate the situation and the circumstances to make the right decision; don't be short-sighted. As you begin what is hopefully going to be a long career in sports, finding the best opportunity or job is far more important than finding the highest paying job. – Ernie Accorsi, former General Manager of the New York Giants.*

Q. Who are the top five most influential people in your career, excluding family, and why?

A. (1) John Hallam (high school coach) – introduced me to Football Ontario.

(2) Howie Starkman (former Public Relations Director for the Toronto Blue Jays) – told me to quit my full-time job and volunteer to gain practical experience.

(3) Charley Casserly (former General Manager for the Washington Redskins and Houston Texans) – offered me a spot in his internship program, and he really took pride in educating the interns who worked for him.

(4) Ernie Accorsi (former General Manager for the New York Giants) – gave me my first full-time job and appreciated the path that I took into the business. He always encouraged my professional growth and challenged me to take on more responsibilities.

(5) Jerry Reese (General Manager for the New York Giants) – allowed me to propose new and creative ideas for our strategic planning. He's very open-minded and willing to explore new concepts. His ability to be fair and firm with everyone breeds loyalty.

Q. When you look to hire someone, what is the most important quality or qualities you look for in an applicant?

A. Confidence in their ability. Competence, work ethic, ambition and a sense of humility. Too often humility is perceived as a lack of self-confidence when in fact, it is a healthy lack of self-preoccupation.

Q. Any guidance with respect to how to secure a position in the sports industry?

A. On the business side, get a job, not an internship. On our side (football operations), there are limited opportunities and many candidates, especially for full-time positions. Identify internships to gain practical experience that is in-line with your career objectives. There is nothing wrong with taking a step back to take three steps forward in the future. It's all about practical experience.

Q. What is your most memorable moment as an employee in the industry?

A. Most memorable moment – our first Super Bowl win. We won the year after Ernie retired, but his fingerprints were all over the organization. He and Jerry Reese positioned our team, the roster and the coaching staff to win a championship.

     *   *   *   *

The business has changed since Kevin's emergence in the National Football League. From an economic standpoint, advances in technology and access to media outlets transformed the economic climate of professional sports. The development of a hard salary cap helped achieve the league parity we see today, which contributed to the economic dominance of professional football. Through all these changes, the responsibilities of league executives have increased. And in addition to the expansion of existing roles within sports, these changes also created the demand for new positions.

Kevin advises that individuals aspiring to work on the operations side of the business should look for practical experience that is in-line with their career objectives. Employing this advice from Ernie Accorsi allowed him to become well-rounded and very good at what he does, which is his key piece of advice to young professionals breaking into the industry.

This is very important, but one of Kevin's best career moves was agreeing to teach the scouting department about the salary cap in exchange for their teaching him how to evaluate talent. He identified his lack of personnel experience as a void in his résumé that could limit his professional potential. In this way, he accounted for this potential shortfall.

Navigating through the front office of a sports organization requires acquiring and refining skills that may not be directly related to your current position. General managers in the National Football League typically ascend the ranks on the operations side of sports with a background in scouting. Kevin started on the right side of the business but lacked the personnel experience he would need if he were going to be more than a Salary Cap Analyst for the New York Giants. His efforts to broaden his scouting aptitude and team building experience put him in position to be considered for the promotion to Assistant General Manager in 2002.

For those looking to work as a salary cap analyst responsible for managing the cap and negotiating player contracts, understanding the Collective Bargaining Agreement (CBA) and the salary cap will open up doors for a position in an NFL front office. This understanding can be developed working outside of sports. The CBA, which is available to the public at no charge, governs how the salary cap operates and sets the parameters that teams and player agents must follow during contract negotiations. Organizations desire a certain level of competence in this area when hiring for an entry-level position in the front office.

Kevin advised that it is incredibly difficult to obtain an entry level, paid position in the area of the salary cap/player contract administration with a professional sports team. Available positions are extremely limited. Professionals looking to obtain their first position must demonstrate their knowledge in this area despite a lack of practical experience, since these positions are so limited. Be creative. Think of changes to the sport or to the overall economics of the league that would impact the salaries of professional athletes. Don't wait for an opportunity to learn these areas of sports business.

Take advantage of the resources that are now readily available to enhance and demonstrate your knowledge.

Once you obtain a position with an organization, Kevin's career path suggests that developing additional skill sets that add value to the organization becomes imperative. For him, the skill set that was lacking was personnel experience. Identify an area of weakness or an emerging need within the organization, and develop your understanding in that area and acquire a new skill set. The potential for a promotion to assistant general manager will then exist.

Pursuing these opportunities prematurely could be a quick ticket out of the organization, while failing to identify these opportunities could result in being overlooked. The key is understanding your role in the organization, performing at a high level and maintaining a good relationship with your manager(s). Ideally they will make these opportunities known to you. If not, it is always recommended to form good working relationships with coworkers in different departments throughout the organization. They may make you aware of these opportunities.

Similar to other positions in sports, there isn't a single universal blueprint that ensures success. Kevin's career path suggests that developing a comprehensive understanding of the industry and the organization will lead to future opportunities. But it isn't realistic to assume everyone has the ability to work various unpaid positions and travel the world for different opportunities without a livable wage. It requires geographic and financial flexibility. On the operations side, the primary points of entry include salary cap, personnel, analytics and sports science/technology. Develop an understanding of one of these areas that will add value to the organization. Once you are a full-time employee, you can broaden your skills by improving your level of proficiency in the others.

6

NFL SCOUT: EVALUATING TALENT AT THE HIGHEST LEVEL

Ethan Waugh – Senior Personnel Assistant for the San Francisco 49ers

"Be seen and not heard. Know your role in the organization, do your job, learn, and when it's your time, have your opinion ready."

The Scouting Combine is one of the hallmarks of the NFL. There is no better place to be in the sports world in the month of February, unless, of course, you are playing in the Super Bowl. If you are looking for a job in the National Football League, attending this event is a must.

I connected with Ethan Waugh, Senior Personnel Assistant for the San Francisco 49ers, while working in the 49ers' front office during the 2011 season. As it turned out, we had more in common than just the same employer. Ethan played football for my uncle, Randy Kuceyeski, in Libertyville, IL, and his father, Maury, coached with my uncle. As an area scout at the time, Ethan was responsible for the Midwest region, and his territory encompassed my previous home and the city where I would return following my tenure with the 49ers.

There is an indoor walkway system that connects the J.W. Marriott, Westin, Hyatt and Convention Center. This walkway serves as the primary route for team executives to navigate downtown Indianapolis in between the workouts at Lucas Oil Stadium and meetings held at each club's respective hotel. From an executive's perspective, the only thing more annoying than getting bombarded with autograph requests is the bitter cold, ice and snow, which Indianapolis is certain to have in the month of February. Team executives use this indoor walkway to avoid these conditions. When I was networking and looking to break into the sports industry, I navigated this indoor walkway a dozen times a day during the NFL Combine.

We met in the corridor flooded with NFL executives and decided to conduct the interview right in the middle of all the action. Ethan has experienced firsthand the technology shift that has occurred in scouting departments all across the NFL. Since he was one of the scouts responsible for this change, I wanted to capture his perspective on where the industry is going and how technology will continue to change scouting. As our conversation wrapped up, I glanced at my watch. The time was 5:30 pm. Ethan had NFL-prospect interviews to conduct. I was excited to begin writing and could only think of one restaurant in downtown Indianapolis to do so.

St. Elmo Steak House is considered THE gathering place during the NFL Scouting Combine. A cozy, renowned steakhouse, St. Elmo was founded in 1902, and as far as I could tell, NFL personnel have been going there since the NFL Scouting Combine relocated to Indianapolis, Indiana, in 1987. Chuck Pagano sat next to me for the first part of my meal; Steve Spagnuolo for the second part. It is rumored that Sean Payton, after winning Super Bowl XLIV, purchased every bottle of wine that Jerry Jones preferred when treating his staff to dinner at St. Elmo every year at the Combine. True to form, Jerry ordered the wine. A note from Sean Payton informed him that his selection was out of stock.

*   *   *   *

Football has always been a huge part of the Waugh family. With three brothers and a father involved in coaching, Ethan had football ingrained in him from an early age. His passion for football guided him to play the sport at a Division III school at the collegiate level.

Ethan finished out his playing career and graduated with a history degree in June of 1997. He knew that he wanted to be a coach, and he assumed his degree in history would help him land a teaching job that most high schools view as a requirement to be a coach. That wasn't the case at first. He remained unemployed and had to make some decisions early in his career. Securing a full time, paid position right out of school is incredibly difficult. He learned about a Graduate Assistant (GA) position at Western Carolina University, a Division I school under head coach Bill Bleil. He interviewed, was offered the position, and accepted the offer to become a graduate assistant. He made $600 per semester in his first paid position in sports.

This opportunity at Western Carolina forced Ethan to learn both sides of the ball and then some. He coached, recruited, scouted and developed student athletes. He began to see every aspect of coaching and started developing the tools necessary to be an effective evaluator of football talent.

He proved himself as a valuable member of the staff while serving as a Graduate Assistant. The coaching staff rewarded him by promoting him to a restricted earnings position.[x] While this was still very low paying, it afforded him certain benefits he did not have as a GA and served as a sign that he was doing the right things early in his career. Ethan continued on this same path and achieved full-time status when a full-time coach left the program and the decision was made to fill this position from within.

After four years at Western Carolina and coming off a 7-4 season in 2001, the entire coaching staff was unexpectedly fired, stemming from incidents involving players and the severity of the players' actions. One player was involved in a shooting; a member of the coaching staff faced legal issues of his own. Ethan wasn't directly involved in any of the incidents bringing negative publicity to the institution, but he was let go. He was 26.

His preference at the time was to remain in football, but professional preferences don't always align with professional opportunities. He understood the importance of finding work while searching for a coaching position. He considered different jobs, including working at a nearby casino. However, he was determined to exhaust any possibility that he would be a coach during the 2001 season before accepting a position outside of sports. Ethan traveled to San Antonio to attend the American Football Coaches Association (AFCA) Convention in hopes of making connections and securing another coaching position.

He used AFCA as an opportunity to connect with coaches and scouts from around the country. One of the people he met up with was Norm Eash, the head coach for Illinois Wesleyan University, who happened to be in the market for a new offensive coordinator. Their meeting led to a job interview and within a month of attending the conference, Ethan was named Illinois Wesleyan's new offensive coordinator.

In this capacity, he was in charge of scouting, game planning, and play calling for the offense. But the job of a collegiate coach is year round and goes well beyond the field. He also spent a great deal of time recruiting and watching film on high school prospects. This is where Ethan began to develop his eye for talent. Whether it was looking to improve a current player's technique or identifying high school prospects, his skills as a scout and talent evaluator really began to take hold.

After two seasons at Illinois Wesleyan, a new opportunity presented itself. He received a phone call from Bill Rees, who at the time was Director of Player Personnel with the San Francisco 49ers and had spoken with him a few months prior. Bill had an entry-level scouting vacancy under him, and he wanted Ethan for the job. His firsthand experience with recruiting and evaluating talent at the collegiate level piqued his interest in this position. What attracted him to this entry-level scouting position was "the opportunity to be around players, coaches and scouts at the highest level of the game."

Recently married, Ethan had to consider whether his wife could endure another drastic career change and geographic relocation. A scouting position in professional football is the exact opposite of a 9-5 office job. Scouts spend a few years in one city, and then bounce from city to city depending on their scouting territory. Once established in the territory, months are spent driving around that territory to evaluate talent and attend various pro days and college games. His wife both understood and supported his passion, and, with her support, he chose to pursue a career as a scout at the highest level of the game.

In the spring of 2004, he officially accepted the job offer. He was 29 years old and now Scouting Assistant for the San Francisco 49ers.

He was presented with a major challenge after his first season in San Francisco, a 2-14 season that lead to the subsequent "house cleaning" of the majority of the front office staff. These proverbial "house cleanings" occur frequently in the NFL, and it is common for clubs to retain a few members from the former staff. The members retained are typically lower on the staff and have an understanding of how the organization operates. It was less than a year since Ethan had joined the 49ers when the person that attracted him to the organization was no longer with the club. As a low man on the totem pole, he was retained, but now he had an entirely new set of bosses to prove himself to and a new set of area scouts to assist with their daily responsibilities.

The scouting offices were way behind when it came to technology, something he took upon himself to address. The 49ers were still using antiquated beta machines to prepare tape and distribute the materials that scouts relied on to evaluate talent. He found himself copying multiple beta tapes to VHS at a time, with different timers monitoring the progress of each tape. Ethan would then FedEx the tapes to the individual area scouts. This process was extremely tedious. But the scouts and executives didn't care how this was done; they only cared about receiving film to review. As Ethan put it, "People don't want to hear about the labor pains. They want to see the baby."

He was an integral part of the organization's migration away from these archaic technologies. Suddenly beta tapes, VHS tapes and even DVDs were a thing of the past.[xi] The scouting professionals located at the Club's home office would copy last season's film and the current season's film to external hard drives and ship them to the area scouts out on the road. This allowed the area scouts to review film while on the road, instead of having to wait until they convened in the Bay area. Ethan's hard work was rewarded with an area scouting assignment.

He was promoted to area scout for the Midwest territory in 2008, where he was responsible for evaluating prospects at various schools, including Ohio State, Michigan, Northwestern, Notre Dame and Michigan State, among others. He would receive scouting assignments and would travel to these institutions to evaluate prospects. NFL clubs, with a few exceptions, belong to one of two scouting partnerships: National Scouting and Blesto. Ethan received baseline grades for college prospects in their final season and subsequently researched and evaluated the prospects in his territory. He prepared and finalized these scouting reports for the organization to review during the pre-Draft process.

Ethan served as the Midwest scout for four years when he was promoted to Senior Personnel Advisor. In this role, he would be involved with scouting processes and the development of scouting tools for the organization, responsibilities he was familiar with thanks to his time as Scouting Assistant. But after transitioning roles to that of an area scout, technological advances continued to transform scouting across the Big Four. Scouting services offered almost instantaneous access to prospect film and the information scouting departments needed to make an informed football decision.

He was, and continues to be, a part of this scouting process transformation. His focus was on streamlining the scouting process to improve the depth of knowledge about each player and, more importantly, how the player would fit in the NFL. These changes that Ethan helped implement were just a start to the scouting system's reworking in San Francisco. His primary responsibilities in San Francisco include maintaining the scouting database, managing the scouting process and evaluating NFL prospects at the collegiate level. Ethan also helps develop software that will continue to improve the scouting process that hopefully will gain them a competitive advantage over other clubs.

*   *   *   *

Q & A: Ethan Waugh's Advice on How to Succeed as a Scout in the Sports Industry

Q. If you could offer some advice to individuals looking to break into the sports industry, what would it be?

A. Be as good to every person that you meet as possible. Not everything is a transaction; personal encounters are valuable in life and provide avenues to seek advice and benefit outside of your direct career path. Stay away from becoming a "what can you do for me" type person.

Q. What is the best piece of professional advice you received during your career?

A. The best professional advice I received as a young person breaking into football was to "be seen and not heard." Know your role in the organization, do your job, learn, and when it's your time, have your opinion ready.

Q. Name one person in the industry that has really helped you along the way.

A. Bill Rees. He opened the door for me and taught me along the way. My emergence in scouting under Bill created a natural network for me.

Q. Who are the top five most influential people in your career, excluding family, and why?

A. Throughout my career, I've tried to take things that certain coaches have done in the locker room or around the office to emphasize the importance of team and sticking together as a collective unit, as opposed to "me" professionals. With this in mind, the top five most influential acts/professionals include:

(1) Todd Berry (Executive Director of AFCA) – He is a big believer in the "work smarter, not harder" philosophy. Thanks to this way of thinking, my brother, who works for Todd Berry, gets home at a relatively normal hour and would ask me, "What are you doing?"

(2) Jim Harbaugh (Head Coach at the University of Michigan) – The dilemma after the 2012 season was whether to focus on the team's accomplishments in 2012, or move on, since the team's personnel had changed drastically. Harbaugh told a story about fighter pilots that keep a kill sign and you are always a part of that. I really reacted to the "this is what the team has accomplished" perspective.

(3) Bill Bleil (Offensive Line Coach for Missouri Southern State University) – He was a big believer in putting the needs of others in front of your own needs. He also stressed the importance of making everyone in an organization feel as though their work is valued. This was evident by the way he treated graduate assistant administrators, viewing them with great respect and considering their input and participation.

(4) Norm Eash (Head Coach for Illinois Wesleyan University) – His primary focus was the importance of attention to detail. He allowed his employees to take on a lot of different responsibilities, but everything had to be done to a certain standard. His motto was "Inspect what you expect."

(5) Brady Hoke (Defensive Coordinator at the University of Oregon) – He played the fight song in the office every day when he was Head Coach at the University of Michigan. That set the tone, established school pride, and reiterated that they are an

organization, and every person has a role that will make the organization better.

Q. When you look to hire someone, what is the most important quality or qualities you look for in an applicant?

A. The typical scouting department has many different personalities with many different backgrounds. The key is finding someone with the social intelligence to be able to identify these different personalities, understand the lingo and convince these individuals that they truly understand the business. I want to find someone that is willing to buy into the organization and accept his/her role in the organization. I strive to avoid those with the "self-promotion" mentality.

Q. How have changes in the industry created additional opportunities for young professionals?

A. There are many different opportunities for people to evaluate talent that didn't exist 5, 10, 15 years ago. The exposure that exists with the introduction of NFL Game Rewind and over 20 different camera views during a live game makes it much easier to identify position-specific abilities and physical traits. Most recently, the NCAA is preparing to open up recruiting and reduce the restrictions on the number of off-the-field staff. The big programs will hire staff just to evaluate talent and scout at the high school level. This will be a great way to develop baseline knowledge to prepare for the next level.

Q. How have advances in technology transformed the applicant pool for potential scouting positions in the National Football League?

A. Advances in technology have impacted scouting departments in different leagues, but it is too difficult to break into a scouting department in the NFL based on one's understanding of technology.

Applicants must have general football knowledge that greatly exceeds the understanding of an everyday fan. It will be obvious to the coaching staff and seasoned scouts if you don't have solid football knowledge.

Q. How has scouting changed since you joined the San Francisco 49ers?

A. In the beginning, the technology aspect (computers, Excel, etc.) of the position was self-taught. You had to be creative and think of ways to get things done quickly and accurately. Now, you need a baseline understanding of how these state-of-the-art systems function. It is still very much about football, just with new or different technology to help evaluate talent.

Q. If you could discourage one type of behavior in a candidate, what would it be and why?

A. I would discourage people from being overly ambitious. I am not discouraging someone from being ambitious, because that is a great quality to have. I am discouraging someone from letting their ambition detract from their daily responsibilities to the organization. Too many people come in thinking that they will be the general manager at 26. I believe that what it takes to be a general manager is learned over time, not through the "I am the smartest person" mentality.

Q. What is your most memorable moment as an employee in the industry?

A. Going to the Super Bowl. Being able to witness the event and the atmosphere.

*   *   *   *

Scouting is a science. The statistics are similar to those of a weatherperson. Scouts are wrong more than they are right, but people forget the times they were wrong when they are right. The personnel decisions of every professional organization are closely scrutinized and publicly criticized. The goal of every scouting department is to gather sufficient information and perform enough work to significantly reduce the margin for error. Technology increases efficiency, which is why these advances have become so important in personnel offices across the Big Four.

While technology has revamped the scouting landscape, the demand still exists for area scouts that cover designated territories across the country. These area scouts still spend an inordinate amount of time on the road and in their cars doing the proverbial "loops" from school to school. Scouting positions now require a level of technology aptitude that didn't exist ten years ago. However, the emergence of technology doesn't eliminate the need for a scout to understand the sport and have an eye for identifying the skills and abilities that translate to the next level.

Ethan's career as a scout started with antiquated scouting tools and progressed to the development of a state-of-the-art scouting system. He taught himself about the changes occurring around the League and used this knowledge to increase his value to the organization. He survived the scouting transformation, but not all scouts were able to adjust to these changes. During our conversation, Ethan continued to stress the importance of understanding one's role within the organization.

I thought about this piece of advice and whether it directly contributed to Ethan's rise in the 49ers' scouting department. He started as an entry-level scout under Bill Rees after years of coaching and recruiting experience. He understood his role at the time, and he continued to deliver a solid work product while making note of the changes taking place across the League. The changes that would have the greatest impact on his profession were right around the corner.

Not only does Ethan understand his role in the organization, but I gathered that he also identifies tasks ancillary to his specific job functions that will teach him an additional skill set and prepare him for other opportunities. His career path exhibits this skill set. One of the advantages of coaching opportunities with smaller universities strapped with budget constraints is the ability to perform your role and learn aspects of other areas related to your role (e.g. coaching and recruiting).

While this approach worked for him, it doesn't come without the risk of being perceived as overly ambitious, a quality he cautions in young professionals looking to advance. It is easy to look past the day-to-day responsibilities in search of more important projects with greater exposure around the organization. Instead, Ethan stresses the importance of understanding your role in the organization and developing skill sets in other areas when the opportunity presents itself.

Becoming a talent evaluator in professional sports requires a unique combination of football knowledge and a baseline understanding of the technology that drives the scouting landscape. Ethan's story suggests that the desire to learn is just as important as the ability to learn. The professionals that understand their role within an organization and learn valuable lessons along the way have a better chance of climbing the ranks in football scouting.

Ethan acknowledged that resources exist today for individuals to insert themselves in a scouting position. Web services offer game film with multiple camera views to evaluate talent. College athletics are expanding the number of staff permitted and designating professionals in scouting capacities. The tools are available to teach yourself about talent evaluation and develop a baseline knowledge that far exceeds the everyday fan. This will position you for an entry-level position interview, where you can display this knowledge.

These opportunities exist, and when one presents itself, make it a priority to *"know your role in the organization, do your job, learn, and when it's your time, have your opinion ready."*

7

CHIEF EXECUTIVE OFFICER: GROUND FLOOR TO THE PENTHOUSE

Derrick Hall – Chief Executive Officer and President for the Arizona Diamondbacks

"Based on my experiences, opportunities at the minor league level provide the greatest training ground possible for professionals to understand what it takes to run an organization."

Director before the age of 30. President by 40. Chief Executive Officer (CEO) before turning 50. Lofty expectations? Not for Derrick Hall.

Derrick started as an intern with the Los Angeles Dodgers' Single-A affiliate. As an intern three leagues removed from Major League Baseball, he learned the business, established an understanding of organizations operating in professional baseball, and developed relationships with coworkers in all areas of the minor leagues and Major League Baseball (MLB). These relationships would prove beneficial as he navigated from intern to a high-level executive with the organization.

I caught an early flight out to Phoenix to catch the second game of a three game series between the Arizona Diamondbacks and the Philadelphia Phillies. I watched the game with Derrick, President and CEO of the Arizona Diamondbacks, and Ken Kendrick, General Partner of the Arizona Diamondbacks. During the course of our interactions, I started to see what it takes to be a successful CEO of a sports organization. This piqued my interest, and I was excited to capture his perspective on the business and learn exactly what it takes to become the CEO of a professional sports franchise.

*   *   *   *

Derrick grew up in Los Angeles in the 1970's and 1980's. The perennial powerhouse Los Angeles Lakers won multiple championships during this period led by Jerry West and Wilt Chamberlain, followed by Kareem Abdul-Jabbar and Magic Johnson. The Los Angeles Dodgers consistently claimed the NL pennant (1974, 1977, 1978, 1981 and 1988) and recorded two World Series trophies in the 1980's.[xii] Professional sports were booming in Los Angeles, and Derrick, a young, impressionable teenager at the time, took notice. He identified at an early age that he wanted to work in sports.

Despite this awareness, he didn't act on it in college. He graduated from Arizona State without a concentration in sports and lacking experience in the industry. Derrick believed that a reputable graduate program would be his ticket into the industry. However, the reputable sports programs demand more than a passion for sport. Prior experience working in the sports industry takes precedence in the admissions process. He was denied admission to Ohio University, among others, early in his career.

He shifted his focus to building his network, which would help him gain this real world experience that graduate programs look for in applicants. He attended the Winter Baseball Meetings in 1991 with this goal in mind. This is an annual event attended by representatives of all 30 Major League Baseball organizations, more than 160 minor league baseball teams, guests from international baseball leagues and executives associated with baseball. If something is going to happen in the offseason in professional baseball, chances are that it either happens at this event or the discussions begin taking place there.

Derrick saw a sign for a party inviting various alumni from Ohio University's Sports Administration to a suite in his hotel. Even though he wasn't invited, he made his way to the party and introduced himself to the Executive Director of Ohio's program, Doc Higgins. Derrick told him that he was previously rejected and felt that they had made a mistake in doing so. Doc Higgins encouraged

Derrick to re-apply but insisted that doing so wouldn't guarantee his admission into the program. He re-applied and was accepted into Ohio University's Sports Administration Program in 1992.

As a result of this early rejection, Derrick was committed to his graduate studies and building his network of sports professionals while at Ohio University. He learned about an internship opportunity through the Ohio University program with the Vero Beach Dodgers, a minor league affiliate of the Los Angeles Dodgers.

He still lacked the practical experience in the industry that most employers viewed as a prerequisite to employment. It was a Single-A affiliate, but it was an opportunity. Derrick was a Dodgers fan and aspired to get back to Los Angeles. This seemed like the perfect starting point. He recalled, "Out of the 25 students in the program at the time, 18 wanted the internship and wanted to work in baseball. But I was determined to get it." Derrick underwent two interviews, including a small group interview with all of the finalists. He was offered the internship and moved to Vero Beach.

He did anything and everything, which enhanced his understanding of the minor leagues. His responsibilities included "running the PA system, stocking the shelves, selling programs and pulling the tarp when it rained." When the on-field promotion (Barney) was a no-show, his wife assumed the role as a big purple dinosaur. He had a short window of time to make a lasting impression on ownership.

He completed his spring training internship and headed out to Phoenix, Arizona, to run an instructional league for the Dodgers. While there, the executive staff in Vero Beach advised a plan to retain Derrick. The executives in Vero Beach were impressed with the relationships he formed with fans, season ticket holders and employees at Dodgertown. He was subsequently named Director of Group Sales for the Vero Beach Dodgers.

He made $16,000 in 1992. While his title was Director of Group Sales, he continued to do just about everything. The minor leagues not only provide an environment where players develop their talents, but these leagues also provide an environment where employees gain experience in just about every area of the organization. While this is true on the business side, the opportunities are a little more limited on the operations side. Luckily for him, the responsibilities bestowed upon employees on the business side with the Vero Beach Dodgers far exceeded the job description at the time of interview. Without such a broad array of responsibilities, Derrick may not have received the advice that has shaped his career path to this day.

He received career advice from various co-workers at the Vero Beach Dodgers. The most influential advice came from Reggie Smith, a former player and field coordinator in Vero Beach. During a six-week instructional league where Derrick served as a business manager and Reggie coordinated the baseball operations, Reggie informed him that his experiences in Vero Beach and his professional strengths were aligned with that of a president of a sports organization, not a general manager. Reggie also informed him that the majority of general managers played baseball at the highest level, an experience that Derrick did not possess.

This valuable career advice and the longevity enjoyed by team presidents and business executives convinced Derrick that this was the path he should take going forward.

While working in Vero Beach, he learned to keep his mouth shut and work hard, and by simply listening and learning, he created his own path out to Los Angeles. He had a favorable reputation among the executive staff with the Los Angeles Dodgers, and it wasn't long before Peter O'Malley, the then-owner and president of the organization, recognized this Director of Group Sales in Vero Beach. Peter eventually named Derrick the Director of Publicity for the Los Angeles Dodgers. He headed west, just as he had set out to do. He was 26.

In this role, Derrick was responsible for all media relations and publicity matters for the organization. Individuals occupying this position traditionally focused on publications, i.e., beat writers, game notes, etc., interviews, and credentialing for the different events. He placed major emphasis on promoting the brand and coaching executives on media training. His approach to this role taught him about the importance of brand placement and the greater business needs of a sports organization.

Derrick was making progress within the organization on the public relations side, but he had a desire to test the waters in the media. His desire along with a period of uncertainty for the organization's management led him to seek available opportunities. He was approached by the Dodgers' flagship radio station to co-host a talk show during the morning commute. Derrick acknowledged, "This was a popular show in the number two market in the country. I had to give it a shot."

In 1999, he served as the talk show host on the Dodgers' station and hosted the Dodgers' pre-game radio show. He was also involved with the local media as the weekend sports anchor for NBC in Los Angeles.

While he enjoyed covering sports, it took approximately one year for Derrick to realize he loved the business side of baseball too much to remain on the media side. When he came to this realization, the Dodgers were looking to hire a new Senior Vice President of Communication. Due to his familiarity with the organization and experience on the business side, he was offered this position in 2000, which he accepted.

Derrick developed and implemented all communications strategies, both baseball and business. He addressed governmental affairs. He also handled broadcasting and game day operations, issued publications and organized community events and affairs. Things were going well for Derrick with the Dodgers.

Unfortunately the same couldn't be said for the ownership structure in Los Angeles. When he started with the organization, the O'Malley family had been a majority owner for over 35 years. Peter O'Malley, who inherited the team from his father Walter O'Malley in 1979, sold the club to Fox Entertainment Group in 1998, and Fox subsequently sold a minority share to Robert Daly in 1999. The ownerships structure changed again in 2004, when the Dodgers were sold to Frank McCourt.

These multiple changes in ownership in LA convinced him to pursue opportunities outside the sports industry. Derrick left for a leadership position with KB Home, which at the time was the nation's fifth-largest homebuilder. He served as Senior Vice

President of Corporate Communications and was tasked with increasing brand awareness for this Fortune 500 Company. Derrick applied the same organizational strategies he used in sports business to his new company. This proved to be successful.

In April of 2005, just one year after leaving the sports industry, Derrick was approached by Ken Kendrick, part-owner of the Arizona Diamondbacks. Ken was strongly considering Derrick for the role of Senior Vice President of Communications. His time away from baseball once again confirmed that Derrick's passion was working in professional baseball. One thing he really missed was the customer service aspect of running a sports franchise. Derrick viewed the customer service aspect in corporate America as "lip service" and acknowledged that "in sports, it can't be."

Derrick decided to return to his passion and accepted the position of Senior Vice President for the Arizona Diamondbacks in May of 2005.

He was very well-versed in Communications and Public Relations early in his career. What he lacked at the time was the business experience necessary to lead a professional sports organization. This changed when the Diamondbacks made him in charge of all business operations. This experience equipped him with the skill sets and business knowledge he needed to take that next step in his career. In September 2006, he was named President of the Arizona Diamondbacks. He was 37.

His first order of business, which he learned extensively when working directly with fans in Vero Beach, was improving fan experience. He viewed fan experience as more than placing a good product on the field. In his mind, fan experience encompasses affordability, cleanliness, entertainment and a wholesome environment.

Derrick improved fan experience by implementing value pricing so fans of all demographics and socio-economic statuses could afford a night at the ballpark. He replaced some of the more expensive merchandise in the team shop with more reasonably priced gear, which proved effective. He also assessed the affordability of concessions, which resulted in a significant price reduction for kids' food and a revised policy that permitted outside food and drink.

He also identified that the office culture needed to be better. Through his work with Peter O'Malley, Derrick became a believer in the concept that if you treat your employees with respect, develop them and recognize them, they, in turn, will treat customers the way customers should be treated.

So he made it a priority to connect with every employee, ranging from game day concession workers to high-level executives. One of his messages shared with these employees was "Find A Way To Say Yes." This customer service philosophy didn't catch on immediately, but it eventually revamped the culture in Arizona. He also encouraged all of his employees to take pride in the organization and to always sell the brand. This required a re-branding of the stadium and the executive offices to send a simpler message to employees.

These changes and his approach to improving the organization worked. Revenues were up 25% since he assumed the role of President. The office culture had improved immensely, and Derrick was always out in the community. He negotiated the Diamondbacks' spring training move and site development with the leaders of the Salt River Pima Maricopa Indian Community. Lastly, he closed a deal with a corporate sponsor that was the most lucrative corporate partnership deal in the Diamondbacks' history at a value of $4 million per year.

This level of success led Ken Kendrick to name Derrick CEO in January of 2009 at the age of 40. He continued to improve the office culture and fan experience. He instituted the Circle of Success, which identifies five critical success factors for the organization: fan experience, performance, community, culture and financial efficiency. He has helped transform the organization into one of the largest philanthropic entities in professional sports.

His focus on community involvement and fan experience has had a positive impact on the bottom line. The Arizona Diamondbacks were worth an estimated $584 million in 2013, a 31% increase from 2012.[xiii] Beyond his direct involvement with the

Diamondbacks, he sits on the MLB's Diversity Committee and the Commissioner's On-Field Diversity Task Force. He continues to build relationships and enhance his understanding of sports business as CEO of the Arizona Diamondbacks. Derrick has succeeded in the sports industry at the highest level, and while his path to this position is important, it's the advice he offers in the following section that pinpoints what skills and qualities are required to become CEO of a professional sports franchise.

*   *   *   *

Q & A: Derrick Hall's Advice on Becoming Chief Executive Officer of a Professional Sports Franchise

Q. How has the industry changed since you started in the business?

A. The biggest change as of late is the increase in digital media and social media. Our organization is constantly under the microscope, and any negative fan experience runs the risk of reaching a greater audience. Twitter and Facebook and Instagram are huge now. Another change is that MLB owns the individual clubs' digital rights (websites). We are starting to see the MLB get more involved with revenue streams that in the past were part of the club's responsibility via local revenue streams.

Q. If you were to hire someone to be your successor as CEO of the Arizona Diamondbacks, what are the skill sets that are required?

A. I would look for someone with a history of treating their employees well and caring for their employees. I've always believed that the customer doesn't come first, the employee does. If you treat your employees with respect, reward, promote, develop them and recognize them, they, in turn, will treat our customers the way we want our customers to be treated.

In this business, you have to realize you won't win every year. You have to be lucky and healthy to win, and it is too easy for people to be volatile and overreact in the industry. I would look for someone with a balanced temperament that understands the business without getting too emotionally involved.

Q. Name one person that helped you break into the industry?

A. My experience with the Vero Beach Dodgers taught me a lot. One person that really provided me with career advice and guidance in Vero Beach was a former player and then-current field coordinator Reggie Smith. While serving as a business manager during an instructional league, Reggie told me that what I wanted to become was president of an organization, not a general manager. Reggie taught me that I still had a lot to learn about the business of baseball.

Q. Your best piece of networking advice?

A. When deciding how often or when to communicate with sports professionals, only communicate with relevant matters and don't force it. Avoid over-communicating and being borderline annoying, because it can backfire. Periodic check-ins are great, but an overabundance of communications should be avoided.

Q. Who are the top 5 most influential people in your career/network?

A. (1) My Father – He was a great player and role model. He taught me to pursue what I love and what I want to do. My dad loved the military, so I almost went to West Point for him. I decided to pursue a career in baseball because my father loved baseball, and this was consistent with his advice.

(2) Reggie Smith (former player and coach for the Los Angeles Dodgers) – Reggie taught me about the business of professional baseball and helped me construct a plan to become what 1 unknowingly desired at the time, which was, in fact, president of an organization. Without his advice, I may have pursued a career as a general manager. Who knows where I would be today had that been the case.

(3) Peter O'Malley (former Owner, President and CEO for the Los Angeles Dodgers) – Peter was by far the most influential person with respect to baseball decisions I've had to make. While I relied on my father for career and personal decisions, I relied on Peter for assistance with baseball decisions.

(4) Bud Selig (former Commissioner of Major League Baseball) – Bud has been a huge part of my career and development as an executive in Major League Baseball. Bud not only acknowledges what I do right, he is also there to offer constructive criticism and advice when I do things wrong.

(5) Ken Kendrick (Part-Owner and Managing General Partner for the Arizona Diamondbacks) – A very smart businessman and entrepreneur. His general intelligence, knack for business, and financial intelligence are second to none. Most importantly, Ken has taught me about business integrity and fiduciary responsibility.

Q.   What is the best piece of professional advice you received during your career?

A.   Treat people right. Peter O'Malley taught me the importance of fans and treating your employees right. While 1 learned this at a young age, my experience with the Vero Beach Dodgers allowed me to connect with the fans in a way that cannot be achieved at the Major League level.

Q. What advice do you have for someone looking to enter a different area of an organization from their current position, similar to your jump from SVP of Communications to President/CEO of the Arizona Diamondbacks?

A. Find a skill set in your current position that transfers to the desired position. For me, my communications skills helped because I already had great relationships with the staff, players and the fans. Also look for a natural fit between your strengths and the demands of the position. To the extent there are gaps, find a way to get that experience. For me, my experience as head of all business operations for the D-Backs filled one of my gaps.

Q. What would you tell aspiring CEOs at the beginning of their career?

A. If you want to become president or CEO of an organization, you almost have to come from the business side. Some organizations have a co-president structure, where one president is from the operations side and the other president is from the business side. This is rare, so understand what you want to become and think of the best way to get there.

Q. What is your most memorable moment in the sports industry?

A. Our 2011 team was picked to be last in the division, but we won the division. That night was unlike any other night I've experienced in 20 years of baseball. Fans were in the pool, everyone went crazy. Utter jubilation. It was great.

Q. What is the one thing that every employer looks for in hiring an employee?

A. I look for a passionate, selfless person that loves the game of baseball. Having a great education will get you an interview, but you can't teach passion and experience. Fitting in with our culture requires a certain level of energy and an optimistic perspective. If you are too concerned with money or the fame in professional sports, your career in sports will likely be cut short.

*   *   *   *

It was the top of the eighth inning. Arizona just took the lead, 3-2, but the Philadelphia Phillies were charging back. A group of Japanese fans approached Derrick. Familiar with their culture, he didn't hesitate to engage in a conversation, even as the Diamondbacks' lead in the game was being threatened. In doing so, he ensured that this group of fans had a great fan experience. This interaction, at a time when the game was on the line, proved that Derrick does more than just preach the culture in Arizona.

It takes a comprehensive understanding of the organization and the business to become the CEO of a sports franchise. Working close to the end consumer in Vero Beach taught him the importance of the fan, and what it would take as an organization to meet fans' expectations. His take is that "there aren't enough people in the business that started out in the minor leagues."

He stressed the importance of minor league positions and dismissed the common misconception that experience in the minor leagues doesn't translate to positions at the major league level. He believes that *"opportunities in the minor leagues provide the greatest training ground possible for professionals."* The key takeaway from my time spent with Derrick and Ken is that executives at the highest level in Major League Baseball can begin their careers in the minor leagues.

Not all minor league opportunities are ideal, and Derrick was sure to acknowledge this. But positions held with minor league organizations that share the same ownership group as its MLB affiliate make it easier to make an impression and jump leagues.

The key is finding or creating the opportunities with these organizations that will teach you what you don't know about a particular area of the business. He acknowledged that one of the keys to becoming CEO of a professional sports franchise is to "find a skill set in your current position that transfers to the desired position and, to the extent there are gaps, find a way to get that experience." He learned almost every aspect of operating a professional sports franchise on a much smaller scale. As he has found out, the lessons he learned in Vero Beach translate to the major league level.

Derrick went on to hold roles in communications, publicity sales and radio. He formed relationships with leaders in the different departments, and before long, he was involved in initiatives that impacted the entire organization. His openness and ability to communicate helped him form strong relationships with members of the Diamondbacks' organization that kept him apprised of the progress in the different areas of the business.

Another takeaway for aspiring CEOs is the importance of creating a sense of passion for the organization with your employees. The CEO is responsible for the bottom line, but focusing exclusively on driving revenue streams that contribute to the bottom line isn't always a successful formula. He or she needs to understand the community and, most importantly, the employees. Derrick acknowledged that when hiring for the organization, he "looks for passionate, selfless applicants that love the game of baseball."

This sense of belonging and love of baseball was evident during my visit and tour of the Diamondbacks' stadium. I spent some time with a fellow alumnus of the Ohio University sports program and current Broadcasting & Multimedia Traffic Specialist for the Arizona Diamondbacks, Leslie Farrell. She, among others, spoke about the great things their organization had accomplished over the years. There was a sense of pride in their voices.

This level of passion was also on display behind the scenes. We took the executive elevator down to the field level and passed various employees. Every employee was greeted with Derrick's fist bump, followed by a quick saying "Drive for Five." The entire organization was in sync. They all appeared happy to be a part of the organization.

It became clear that this passion shared by the employees in Arizona stems from the corporate culture in Arizona and Derrick's commitment to employees of the organization. This was most evident after Derrick was diagnosed with prostate cancer in September 2011. Shortly after the diagnosis, he entered his office and discovered that the organization created the slogan "DHall....Dbacks" and printed it on rubber wristbands. The entire organization stood behind him. His level of caring and passion was not only recognized and appreciated, it was reciprocated.

His success in Arizona and rapid ascension in professional baseball led sports executives and media sources to peg him as the successor to Bud Selig as the next Commissioner of Major League Baseball. This is high praise for a professional working on the team side of Major League Baseball that lacked experience working on the League side of the business. Rob Manfred, an MLB executive with numerous years of experience working for Major League Baseball, was named as Selig's successor on August 14, 2014, putting any speculation on Derrick's future status as Commissioner to bed.[xiv] Regardless of where his next step lies, he will get there by building relationships, understanding the business, and developing a sense of passion and affiliation, both within the organization and in the surrounding community. Derrick's successor in Arizona will need to do the same.

8

SPORTS MARKETER: SPONSORSHIPS, INNOVATION, AND FAN ENGAGEMENT

Brian Gainor – Vice President of Innovation at Property Consulting Group

"When launching a career in sports, the most valuable thing you can do is identify people to work for that believe in you, challenge and empower you, and help you see the world differently. These are the type of mentors you want to have in place that will ultimately put you in the best position to succeed in life."

Fans enjoy witnessing the half-court shot at basketball games, but how many remember the presenting sponsor of that shot? Or who can name the company behind the popular hot dog run at the local ballpark? The larger answer to these questions is driving engagement and brand awareness.

Sports enthusiasts watch live sporting events because they love to be entertained as part of a fun, action-filled communal viewing experience. As sports have matured over the years, so has the entertainment value of the live viewing experience and the role that sponsors can play in enhancing that experience for fans. The key to success is understanding exactly who fans are (their segmented profiles, interests, and behaviors), being able to think like them, and developing creative, memorable experiences that change the way they think, feel, and behave. As a sports marketer and fan engagement strategist, Brian Gainor helps teams, leagues, and organizations worldwide better understand, build, engage, and monetize their fan bases (of all ages) and creatively partner with sponsors to deliver value and entertainment in new, innovative ways.

The greatest asset a sports property has is its relationship with its fans.

To learn more about this side of sports business, I met Brian at Mickey Finn's Brewery, a small local brewery located in Libertyville, Illinois. One thing is certain, success in this field does not always require being the first to introduce a new fan engagement idea or sponsorship strategy. The most successful sports marketing ideas are often a combination of several creative ideas developed and implemented by teams, leagues, and brands around the world. The key to success is taking these ideas, molding them (specific to your challenge or opportunity), and creatively bringing them to life through online and offline channels. Doing this successfully will result in reaching, engaging and impacting fans around the world.

Having a passion for identifying unique sports marketing ideas and improving upon them is what led Brian to create Partnership Activation, a sports business website that specializes in sharing sports marketing and sponsorship best practices from around the world. Since its launch, Partnership Activation has become a leading destination for thousands of teams, brands and agency marketers to visit for inspirational ideas, industry trends and creative solutions.

His contributions in the world of sports business and social media earned him a spot on Forbes' Top 30 Under 30 list in 2011, a distinction he shares with LeBron James, Jonah Hill and Jennifer Lawrence, among others. Brian's efforts have helped teams, leagues and organizations better engage fans and activate leading brand partners, while improving the most important brand of all. His own.

*   *   *   *

Brian Gainor's pursuit of a career in sports all started with a long daily walk past Ben Hill Griffin Stadium, commonly referred to as "The Swamp", during his freshman year at the University of Florida. As a business major, Brian had never given much thought to working in sports until he found himself incredibly intrigued by all that he saw and heard during his daily walks to and from class, including student-athletes running practice drills, massive stadium construction projects, and passionate fans admiring statues of Gator legends outside the iconic college football venue.

This exposure during his first few semesters on campus led him to seek opportunities at the University of Florida's Sports Information Department (SID). Following the advice of an esteemed professor on campus, Brian sought to volunteer within the University Athletic Department to get as much experience as possible as a student. While his initial pursuits came up short within the university, his conversations led him to the Sports Information Department, which had an open-door policy allowing students that aspire to work in the sports industry to find volunteer work.

He immediately signed on to be a Media Relations Assistant and was responsible for covering games, conducting interviews, writing features, and tracking statistics for a variety of men's and women's sports. There, he met a number of other passionate students and university employees with similar career aspirations.

His experiences as a young student at the University of Florida led him to apply for an internship with the Miami Dolphins as a Training Camp Operations Assistant during his sophomore year. At the time, the Dolphins organization offered a comprehensive summer internship program for junior and graduating senior college students that provided an inside look at life working in professional sports. Brian's SID experience was something that distinguished him from other applicants. Despite the fact that he was a sophomore and the Dolphins' internship was historically given to juniors and seniors, Brian applied and offered multiple references that supported his candidacy for the internship position. He went through the formal interview process with the organization and was hired as a Training Camp Operations Assistant.

Brian and a team of others were responsible for managing all aspects of the fan experience at the Dolphins' training camp. This included youth activities, VIP check-in, marketing initiatives and promotional activities.

Brian's experience working for the Dolphins heightened his passion for working in sports and inspired him to actively seek out additional internships and volunteer opportunities during his final two years at the University of Florida, including working at the Orange Bowl, SEC basketball tournaments and more. These opportunities allowed Brian to gain additional real-world experience, expand his network of contacts and friends in the industry, and aligned nicely with his winter and spring breaks from classes.

In 2003, Brian met a fellow UF SID student assistant Patrick Smyth, who was interning with the Tampa Bay Buccaneers' Public Relations department. Patrick took Brian under his wing and helped him land an official internship with the Buccaneers as a Public Relations Assistant during his junior and senior years, an opportunity that would prove monumental for his career.

With the Buccaneers, Brian was tasked with providing support during training camp and on game days with press clippings, player interviews, press conferences, website features and other duties as assigned. He was thrilled to have received an offer to work for the Buccaneers organization, even if it meant waking up at 5:00 a.m. on Sunday mornings to drive two hours to work game days, only to make the two-hour drive back to campus later that night.

During his final year as an undergraduate student at the University of Florida, Brian realized that he wanted to emulate the career path of several administrators working in the University of Florida's Athletics Department. He applied to several leading sports graduate programs in the nation, including Ohio University, in furtherance of his desire.

While doing so, he leveraged key relationships that he cultivated and maintained with several Buccaneers PR executives to learn about and ultimately land a job as a U.S. Public Relations Assistant for the Rhein Fire of NFL Europe, based in Dusseldorf, Germany. After several conversations with NFL Europe executives 1 the months leading up to his graduation, it was hard to pass up an)portunity to move abroad and experience the NFL's international)wth initiatives firsthand.

Brian served as the primary point of contact for NFL teams allocated players to play in the league. He traveled with the throughout Europe, gaining a new, unique perspective and ciation for the international sports landscape. The opportunity to work and travel abroad at a young age provided an invaluable perspective of the different ways fans follow and engage with sports around the world and new, unique growth opportunities, largely from a sponsorship and marketing standpoint. This experience allowed Brian to develop a unique lens of the international sports marketplace that has guided his entire career.

While working in NFL Europe, Brian learned that he had been accepted into the Sports Administration program at Ohio University, the top-ranked program in the world offering an MBA/MSA curriculum. Following the conclusion of the 2005 NFL Europe season, Brian flew straight to Athens, Ohio, to begin summer coursework and a new chapter in life.

Brian came to realize while at Ohio University that his true passions, interests, and skillsets were best suited for the world of sports marketing, not public relations and communications. His participation in Ohio's graduate program provided him with opportunities to gain real-world, industry experience working on revenue generation projects for leading brands investing in sports sponsorships. One project in particular solidified his interests and career pursuits. Brian helped develop and present a "Miller Lite Power Play" promotional concept that provided him with a core foundation in sports marketing and sponsorships, which ultimately led him to seek out a career as a brand marketer.

He enhanced his networking skills and, through this process, developed close relationships with several alums of the Ohio University Sports Administration program who worked at GMR Marketing on the Miller Lite business, among others. These relationships led to an exciting internship opportunity (and a foot in the door) with GMR, a leading global experiential marketing agency specializing in helping brands leverage sports, music, and entertainment to engage fans.

Brian joined GMR as part of the agency's internal Sports Consulting Group and was responsible for supporting a number of clients with sponsorship trends, insights, and ideas. He worked under an incredible team of personal mentors that taught him the business and helped him professionally. This introductory experience led

Brian to realize that when it comes to getting your first job in sports, "who" you work for is far more important than "where" you work.

After several months, he was given an opportunity to transition over to client management, where he helped ING and Lowes develop and manage their sponsorship portfolios and activation strategies, spanning soccer, football, college athletics, theme parks and more. These experiences helped Brian learn the fundamentals of developing, executing, and measuring holistic sponsorship marketing programs and truly understanding how to effectively reach and engage fans.

During his early years at GMR, Brian continually sought out new ways to create value and differentiate himself, expand his network, and work to become a recognized thought leader in sports. These aspirations led him to launch a website designed to share creative sports marketing and sponsorship ideas and best practices across the globe. At the time, there were a very limited number of resources for sports business professionals worldwide to use to network, find, and share creative sponsorship, marketing, and fan engagement ideas.

After several weeks of planning, he sought out individuals who helped him launch the site, www.PartnershipActivation.com, and used early mornings, late nights, and weekends to research, identify, and post compelling sports marketing and sponsorship ideas, trends, and insights. Brian utilized contacts in his personal network, team websites, industry databases, social channels, and targeted email outreach to drive traffic and establish a loyal following for the content featured on the site. But while the site's traffic picked up, so did his responsibilities at GMR. He was also approached with new opportunities speaking at industry conferences and writing for CNBC's Sports Biz column. During that time, Brian continually made it a priority to put his work responsibilities first and his related career passions second.

As Brian's career progressed, he took the advice of some industry colleagues and became an early Twitter adopter. He actively used the platform to share insightful articles, ideas, and nuggets of information to followers and fellow industry professionals. This helped him grow the Partnership Activation Platform to reach 8,000+ sports business professionals across 80+ countries. In doing so, he created a Partnership Activation Rising Stars platform designed to recognize and unite the next generation of leaders in sports business under the age of 30.

Brian continued to work hard and distinguish himself in the sports marketing field. Over the course of three years, he was given additional opportunities to develop strategies and manage property relationships for clients and received an opportunity to move to Milwaukee, Wisconsin, to work out of GMR Marketing's global headquarters in 2010.

The move appealed to Brian, as it provided an opportunity to get extensive sports sponsorship and media experience working on the agency's Comcast business, a leading telecommunications company with a diverse sponsorship portfolio spanning the majority of the major sports leagues in the United States. During this time, Brian helped the brand develop and launch an industry-leading sports social media strategy tied around a promotional initiative that allowed fans to win "The Ultimate Sports Social Media Job" and involved a series of team, league, and network partners.

After several years developing and managing sponsorship and social media programs for Comcast, Brian received an opportunity to help launch and lead a new division of GMR Marketing called Freshwire. In this role, he specialized in helping brands effectively create and distribute compelling, unique content for fans. The new role enabled him to stretch far outside his comfort zone, working with clients on projects largely outside the realm of sports and entertainment, and creating new concerted opportunities to reach the right fan at the right time with the right message. This experience helped Brian develop a new set of entrepreneurial skills, look at the sports industry from "the outside in" and create new forward thinking content ideas for clients and the sports industry as a whole.

He also learned to leverage digital media to reach new fan bases and make sponsorships more effective. Working on initiatives outside of sports, this experience confirmed what Brian already knew. He wanted to get back to working directly in sports. GMR was looking to hire someone as Director of Global Sports and Entertainment Consulting, so Brian submitted his name for consideration.

His relationships with various professionals at GMR and experience in different areas of the organization made him a qualified candidate, and he had an opportunity to accept a position on the team.

Brian acknowledged, "This was a tremendous career move because it allowed me to use my collective experience working on the team side and agency side to consult some of the world's largest brands and their partnerships with the NFL, MLB and the Olympics." He assisted BP with its athlete endorsements in the Olympics and Paralympics and consulted The Hartford on its official league partnership with Major League Baseball. He also assisted international sports brands like Manchester City grow their brand and fan base in the United States.

He went on to serve as the Director of Global Sports and Entertainment Consulting for GMR Marketing until November of 2015, when he accepted a new role as Vice President of Innovation for the Property Consulting Group (PCG), a leading global sports innovation and fan engagement company based in Chicago, Illinois.

Brian and the PCG team specialize in helping teams, leagues, and organizations worldwide develop breakthrough ideas, strategies, and solutions, spanning sponsorship, marketing, ticketing, and fan engagement. As the sports world moves at the speed of digital, PCG helps sports properties worldwide creatively generate new revenue streams, solve big problems, and capitalize on blue ocean opportunities.

Times are rapidly changing in the world of sports business and the PCG Innovation team, led by Brian and Dan Migala, are on the forefront helping sports organizations worldwide build and engage the next generation of fans, become truly global brands, and create new, breakthrough sponsorship inventory and ideas. While just 32 years of age, Brian has already made a big impact on the sports business industry and the best is yet to come.

*   *   *   *

Q & A: Brian Gainor's Advice on Becoming a Sports Marketing Professional

Q. How has the industry changed since you started in the business?

A. The sports landscape has changed dramatically since I first entered the sports industry, largely due to the role and impact that social media and new technologies have had. Fans are more connected and more in control than ever before. It's an amazing time to be working in sports as we help traditionally "national" sports organizations become truly global brands and create new, memorable touchpoints and experiences for fans all around the world.

Q. If you were to hire someone to do exactly what you do, what are the skill sets that are required?

A. When hiring, I look for individuals who are passionate, eager to learn, reliable, humble, honest, and have all the qualities you look for in a rock star teammate. I want to surround myself with people who are inspiring, smart, creative, goal-driven, and passionate about what they do.

Q. Name one person that helped you break into the industry?

A. I can't point to just one person. However, I have to say that having the opportunity to be a part of the Ohio University Sports Administration program was a game changing moment in my career, as it helped me develop my strongest friendships (in sports and in life) and has opened up an endless amount of doors and unique experiences.

Q. Your best piece of advice?

A. My best advice for aspiring sports business professionals would be to think of yourself as a brand, identify and act on your core strengths and passion points, gain as much experience as fast as you can, network and learn something new every day, and do all the little things that make a big difference.

Q. Who are the top 5 most influential people in your career/network?

A. (1) John Gainor (my father and CEO of International Dairy Queen) – For the past 32 years, my dad has taught me the importance of working hard, treating everyone with respect, being true to yourself, investing time in your family, and being humble.

(2) Jan Katzoff (former Head of GMR's Global Sports & Entertainment Consulting Practice) – Jan is the most gracious leader I've ever had an opportunity to work for. He taught me how to lead with passion, integrity, transparency, and focus and truly made a difference in so many people's lives. I'll forever be indebted to Jan for paving the way, believing in me, and showing me how to live life to the fullest.

(3) Dan Migala (Co-Founder and Chief Innovation Officer of Property Consulting Group) – Dan has played an instrumental role in my life as a friend, colleague, and visionary in sports. Dan has helped me realize that you can dream big and pursue greatness while balancing and prioritizing time with family. Dan is one of the most creative and innovative minds I've ever met, but the thing I'll always appreciate about him most is the way he approaches life, business, and his relationships with friends and family.

(4) Jim Kahler (Executive Director of Center for Sports Administration at Ohio University) – Since graduate school, Jim has

been an incredible mentor who has helped me navigate the sports marketplace and is always available to lend a helping hand.

(5) Shawn Amos (former CEO of Freshwire) – Shawn is the most inspirational person I've ever had a chance to work for. He lives life with passion, treats people right, and truly values and utilizes his talents (in both business and music) to the fullest.

Q. What is the best piece of professional advice you received during your career?

A. Focus on everything you are doing now and the future will take care of itself. You must be willing to remain flexible with constant, unexpected change in the sports industry and always look to push the envelope, think differently, and challenge the status quo.

Q. What is your most memorable moment in the sports industry?

A. My favorite moment working in sports was having an opportunity to take my grandfather, Gorge, a lifelong Notre Dame fan, to see his first game live in South Bend, IN. It was an incredible weekend experience with my family that I'll always remember and a simple reminder of the lifelong memories we can create for all fans around sporting events worldwide.

Q. Name a particular experience or event that had a great impact on your career.

A. During my first few months interning with GMR Marketing, I learned a life lesson that helped reshape the way I approach work, contributing value, and differentiating oneself within an organization. As a recent hire, I came to work every day doing what was asked of me and not much more. I soon was given feedback that I needed to pick up my performance, ask more questions, add more value, and proactively offer to help others within the agency or else I wouldn't be around too long. Upon receiving this feedback, I really begin to focus, network, work longer hours, position myself as an expert within the company (around activation), and go above and beyond. That was truly a moment that has helped motivate me throughout my career,

Q. How do you foresee technology changing the industry moving forward?

A. Technology will continue to play a major role in the sports industry as teams, leagues, and brands look to bring fans closer and more connected to the live action, their favorite players, coaches, mascots, cheerleaders, and more. Technology will enable teams to better build deeper relationships with fans across the world and provide new ways for fans to be empowered, involved, and engaged for life.

*   *   *   *

View yourself as a brand, and build your brand based on your core strengths and passion points. I'm paraphrasing, but this was the core philosophy behind Brian's best piece of advice. I thought about his advice and how it applies in his career as a sports marketer. His focus on the individual as a brand is unique, but it has helped him achieve tremendous success early in his career. He did just this when he launched www.partnershipactivation.com, but more importantly, he did this when building his network in the sports industry, which has contributed to his success at GMR and with his website.

Brian said two things that really stood out in my mind. His first piece of advice applies across all industries and is generally overlooked by most people. He stated, "When launching a career in sports, the most valuable thing you can do is identify people to work for that believe in you, challenge and empower you, and help you see the world differently. These are the type of mentors you want to have in place that will ultimately put you in the best position to succeed in life."

*   *   *   *

owie's love of sports started early. He would drag his family
ers to sporting event after sporting event. Despite his
tence and their involvement in athletics through Howie, his
y never really took to sports, but they continued to support his
sts. He expressed enough interest in sports for the entire family.
His passion for sports continued through middle school and
school. Howie took it upon himself and began studying sports,
yzing the various NFL Draft results, and learning the NFL's
iness model. He would watch college and professional football
mes with a notebook on his lap and evaluate different players. He
s fascinated with how sports dynasties and successful
ganizations were built. He paid particularly close attention to the
985-1986 New York Mets and the Chicago Bears, but he also
acked the personnel moves of the New York Giants and the New
York Jets. He did this for years leading up to his high school
graduation. He enrolled at the University of Florida and pursued his
BBA in political science. This was the first step towards his law
degree, which he intended to use to break into the NFL.

Howie had very little experience in sports as a freshman at
Florida. He told his college roommate, Jedd Fisch, that he would be a
general manager in the NFL. Jedd chuckled. Jedd Fisch told him that
he would be a head coach in the NFL. Howie laughed.

He continued evaluating talent in his notebooks and learning
everything he could about professional football. He taught himself
about the different personnel schemes in professional football. His
roommate helped with this aspect of the learning curve. This was the
extent of his involvement in the sports industry at the time of
graduation. He stayed on track and pursued his law degree at
Fordham.

Howie identified that it would be incredibly difficult to get into
football operations without some type of scouting experience in the
industry, so he considered the different paths he could pursue with a
law degree to secure an entry-level position in operations and

Too much emphasis is often placed on the job title and the level
of responsibility. It is human nature to focus on the position itself
and fail to consider the people that are responsible for the success of
the position. Do your research. Form strong relationships with
professionals whose careers you would like to emulate. Build these
relationships and convince them that it is in their best interest to have
you work for them. This is simpler said than done, but my strategies
put forth in the final chapters should assist you along the way.

The second takeaway from Brian's interview has limited
application and pertains to a career in sports marketing and
sponsorship consulting. In order to succeed as a professional in
sports marketing and sponsorship consulting, effectiveness is more
important than ingenuity. Understanding the consumer is often as
simple as capturing existing ideas/strategies and repurposing them.

Brian was exposed to different ideas and marketing concepts
that most people in the industry were not privy to prior to the
creation of his website. His willingness to travel expanded his
creative horizons through his exposure to branding concepts
overseas. He also identified that the lack of sharing of sponsorship
ideas across the sports industry actually hurts professionals working
in corporate sponsorships and the brands they represent. The idea
behind Partnership Activation was to share these ideas that have
proven success in a niche market or particular culture.

Brand marketing is arguably more important today than it has
ever been. Today's consumers control the content that they view on a
daily basis. Social media makes it possible for consumers to pick and
choose, a luxury that didn't exist 10 years ago. As such, brands are
fighting for consumer attention. Experts in the field of sports
marketing and sponsorship consulting are in a position to help these
brands.

Brian has relied on his different roles in his career, his network
and his website to capture the attention of professionals in his field.
His status as a member of Forbes' Entertainment Top 30 Under 30
enhances his personal brand, a brand he's been polishing since his
time at the University of Florida. But most importantly, his network,
his website and now, his personal brand help him develop concepts

and marketing practices that catch the eyes of consumers. And in sports marketing, fan engagement and sponsorship consulting are all that matters.

9

GENERAL MANAGER: RUNNING T.

*Howie Roseman – Executive Vice President of Foo
for the Philadelphia Eagles and former General M.
Philadelphia Eagles*

*"How you deal with an issue defines you, so you must
for things that come up."*

A seven-year-old boy sporting a New York Yank
quietly in his seat on his first airplane ride. The head
premier collegiate institution's football program was seated
ahead of that seven-year-old boy. Fate would have it that th
them ended up side-by-side for the trip. They talked footh
everything there was to know about the game. It also came
the coach's son was a member of the Yankees, a fact that surfa
reference to the boy's hat. The seven-year-old boy was H
Roseman. The college coach was Jack Elway, head football coac
Stanford University.

As he deboarded the airplane, Jack Elway handed the boy
mother a business card and asked her to have Howie call him whe
he graduated high school. He opined that Howie knew more about
football than most adults and any other seven-year old boy he had
ever met. While Jack's business card was misplaced over the years,
Howie's intentions of becoming a general manager in the National
Football League were not. Time would prove Jack Elway's intuition
correct. Howie was named General Manager of the Philadelphia
Eagles on January 29, 2010.

eventually become a general manager. One such area, at the time, was the salary cap.

During law school, he remained focused on his law school studies while he also learned everything he could about the NFL's salary cap during his free time. He studied the CBA and taught himself how the CBA provisions governed NFL player contracts and the salary cap. He also relied on relationships he had formed along the way and conversations with these individuals to learn more about the business, specifically football operations.

He did not volunteer or work in sports during law school, but he made it a priority to reach out to every NFL team and express his interest in working on the operations side of the business. He started a letter writing campaign, hoping that just one team would give him an interview. In his letter, Howie introduced himself and communicated his passion for sports, making certain that the recipients understood he was willing to volunteer if necessary. He was persistent and stuck with this approach until he started hearing back from NFL clubs.

Howie received feedback and a response from a few clubs, but most of his letters went unacknowledged. The first team that responded in a favorable manner was the New York Jets. Mike Tannenbaum, who at the time was the Assistant General Manager, responded to Howie's request for an opportunity as an intern. His reason for responding to his email, according to Howie, "You wrote me thank you notes for rejection letters. Anyone that passionate and persistent deserves an interview."

He interviewed with Mike Tannenbaum and Head Coach/General Manager Bill Parcells at the New York Jets' facility. The interview process included a scouting project that would display Howie's knowledge of player personnel and his ability to evaluate talent. Coach Parcells asked him to identify the position that he knew best and the position he knew the least about. His response to the latter question was defensive line.

Coach Parcells tasked him with evaluating various defensive linemen for him to review. He had approximately one week to review the top ten defensive linemen in the upcoming NFL Draft.

Howie prepared a strengths and weaknesses assessment for each prospect, along with an elaborate summary. This was his chance to display his ability to evaluate talent at the highest level.

The competition for this position was stiff. He did not receive feedback from Coach Parcells on the scouting project that he submitted. Ultimately, the position was offered to another applicant who previously served as the Jets' then-current Offensive Coordinator's graduate assistant.

Howie shifted his focus to the other 31 teams. Joe Banner was the President for the Philadelphia Eagles, and he had received Howie's letters seeking an opportunity with the organization. Based on his unfounded assertion that the New York Jets recommended him for a position with the organization if one were available, Joe Banner's assistant passed along his information. Joe spoke with Mike in New York. While both were convinced that Howie was more of a stalker than an aspiring general manager, Joe decided to give him a chance.

Following his graduation from law school and sitting for the bar exam, Howie was hired as an intern for the 2000 season at the age of 24 without any promise of a full-time job at the expiration of the season.

He accepted the position with great enthusiasm. His parents didn't share this same level of enthusiasm. The job was unpaid. Howie lived in New York. He had law school loans that would require repayment in the near future. These circumstances made it difficult to work for free, but he remained committed to breaking into the National Football League. This was the first step.

He woke up every morning at 4:30 a.m. in New York City. In order to get into the Eagles' offices by 8:00 a.m., he had to catch the 5:15 a.m. train. He would work until 7:00 p.m., followed by a two-hour commute back to New York City. He was commuting four hours a day and working eleven.

Howie worked on the side of an administrative assistant's desk. He always asked a lot of questions, so, to him, sitting at the side of someone's desk that was surrounded by front office executives was rather convenient. His responsibilities were limited to the salary cap and issues related to player contracts. He had nothing to do with scouting or player personnel, so he found himself learning everything he could about the salary cap to become an expert in his specific role with the organization. Howie was breaking down NFL player contracts, analyzing the market for different positions, assisting with managing the Eagles' cap and cash positions and keeping an eye on the Eagles' future cash commitments and salary cap ramifications.

Once he finished everything he had on his plate for that day, he would stick around the office and teach himself about personnel matters. He also listened to the conversations between scouts and the Eagles' personnel directors to learn the lingo and better understand talent evaluation. Howie wanted to put himself in a position to be considered for a full-time job following the 2000 NFL season.

Howie approached Joe Banner and said, "I need to know if the Philadelphia Eagles are going to hire me full time. Otherwise, I am going to start looking for full-time opportunities with one of the other 31 teams." He recalls being very considerate during his approach. He had very little leverage to demand a full-time position, but Howie wanted Joe to understand how passionate he was about the Eagles and becoming a big part of the organization moving forward.

Shortly thereafter, Howie was offered a full-time position by the Philadelphia Eagles. He was named Salary Cap Analyst/Staff Counsel in 2001.

Unbeknownst to him at the time, he would remain with the Philadelphia Eagles for his entire professional career as of the publication of this book. In 15 seasons, Howie climbed the ranks in the organization and served in many different roles, culminating with his being named General Manager for the Philadelphia Eagles on January 29, 2010. He remained in this role until January 2, 2015.

He went from intern to general manager in ten years. At the age of 34, he became the youngest general manager in the National Football League. He witnessed some of the organization's greatest challenges and opportunities. Howie witnessed the signing and eventual departure of well-known wide receiver Terrell Owens. He orchestrated the plan to acquire the media-labeled "Dream Team" in the 2011 offseason.[xv] When the Eagles decided to part ways with long-time head coach Andy Reid, it was Howie that was highly involved with the national search to identify Andy Reid's replacement. His tenure as general manager displays what it takes to go from someone with very little experience in the industry to the leader of a professional sports organization.

Jack Elway passed away on April 15, 2001. Howie wrote Jack's wife Jan a letter, thanking Jack for believing in him. The conversation that Jack had had with Howie so long ago equipped him with the confidence he needed to become a General Manager in the National Football League. From that day forward, he stuck to his plan and achieved what he set out to accomplish.

*   *   *   *

Q & A: Howie Roseman's Advice on Becoming a General Manager in the National Football League

Q. Name the top three qualities that a general manager of a professional sports team must possess?

A. It is difficult to identify specific qualities, but it is important to (1) ensure you have good people around you so that you aren't spread so thin, (2) remain organized and detail oriented, and (3) have a vision and, more importantly, a plan to get to that vision.

Q. What do you caution as a new employee approaching a general manager?

A. You must be careful that your aspirations and your goals don't get in the way of what's expected of you. You must develop patience and understand that there are ways to do things while being respectful of the process without stepping on others' toes.

Q. As a general manager, what other areas do you have to be knowledgeable in other than personnel?

A. You watch tape and evaluate players, but you also interact with the different team leaders, fans, media, etc. You are constantly under intense media scrutiny and portraying the organization in a positive light.

Q. How has the industry changed since you started in the business?

A. I think the responsibilities have changed because of social media sites, such as Twitter, Instagram and other media platforms. Things that used to be not such a big deal you now have to be able to react and figure out on the fly because so many people have access to information.

Q. For aspiring general managers, how do you recommend they gain the experience necessary to one day be named general manager?

A. Become an expert in your specific area before you even explore learning other areas. Make sure the organization is very happy with the work you are supposed to be doing before you ask questions about a position or skill set that you hope to acquire.

Q. If you were to hire someone to be your successor as GM of the Philadelphia Eagles, what are the skill sets that are required?

A. I would look for someone with intelligence, persistence and determination. A person willing to sacrifice, think outside the box and that has a feel for people.

Q. Name one person that helped you break into the industry.

A. Mike Tannenbaum – He gave me my first interview and subsequently helped me handle being a general manager in a big market. His advice and knowledge gained through his personal experiences helped me throughout my career.

Q. What is your best piece of networking advice?

A. Talk to as many people in your field as you possibly can. If you are determined and have a passion for a field, do not let anyone tell you NO. Continue to develop your network, work hard, and become as well rounded as possible so when you get an opportunity in that field (internship or a job), you are off and running.

Q. How do you recommend approaching and networking with general managers and other high-level executives?

A. It is a difficult balance between being respectful and being persistent, so make sure you acknowledge that this is a privilege, not a right, and express appreciation for their time.

Q. Who are the top 5 most influential people in your career/network?

A. (1) Jeffrey Lurie (Owner of the Philadelphia Eagles) – Jeffrey is an unbelievable person to work for, very supportive, and asks intelligent questions that make me better at my job. Jeffrey trusted me with his organization and has been a great person to be around and work for since I started in the industry. I can't thank him enough and want to win a championship for him!

(2) Andy Reid (Head Coach for the Kansas City Chiefs) – He is the best leader I've ever been around. He is a great person, he

taught me how to treat people, and he placed great trust in me with different opportunities that advanced my career.

(3) Joe Banner (former President for the Philadelphia Eagles) – Joe is incredibly bright and the way his mind works is like going to graduate school. He is a very intelligent person with innovative ideas and outside-the-box thoughts. I can't thank him enough for all the opportunities and insight he gave me.

(4) Tom Heckert (former General Manager for the Philadelphia Eagles) – Tom gave me the opportunity to go on the road and scout. I am appreciative of the amount of patience he showed and time spent to help me learn the business. He taught me the day-to-day decisions and responsibilities of a general manager.

(5) Ryan Grigson (General Manager for the Indianapolis Colts) – Ryan supported me when I was named General Manager and served as a chief advisor on and off the field. I could always count on him for an honest opinion, which was invaluable over the years. He has done a great job as General Manager of the Indianapolis Colts.

Q. What is the best piece of professional advice you received during your career?

A. Master the area that you are in and try to become an expert in one field before you go on to the next one. This is the philosophy of the Philadelphia Eagles' organization.

Q. What would you tell someone that gets a late start in the industry, but aspires to be a General Manager in the National Football League?

A. A career on the operations side of the business is very difficult to obtain without prior experience in the field. You must be willing to sacrifice weekends and time with family to get the initial experience you need to make a name for yourself in the industry.

Q. What has been the biggest challenge during your tenure with the Philadelphia Eagles?

A. Dealing with the Terrell Owens situation following our Super Bowl run. The team experienced so much success from 2000-2004, so Terrell's departure was my "welcome to the NFL" moment. This taught me that how you deal with an issue defines you, and you have to have a plan for things that come up.

*   *   *   *

Long before Howie was named General Manager for the Philadelphia Eagles, he had a plan. He made it clear during our conversations that executives at the highest level must demonstrate an ability to develop and execute a plan. According to him, "The best time to prepare and develop a plan to address different situations is during down time before events transpire so that you remain disciplined during the intense moments." Howie's pursuit of a career in the NFL displayed this ability.

He also acknowledged that you can't always foresee events that will allow you enough time to develop a plan. Consider the various sports controversies that have surfaced and sparked debates, wreaking havoc for general managers: video of an NFL player using a racial slur, information leaked in New Orleans that resulted in Bountygate, and elevator video footage that captured a domestic dispute involving a prominent NFL player.

Howie opined, "While the industry is very competitive, as a general manager you are part of an elite level of professionals that respect and appreciate others that have risen to the same level. This level of respect is what drives these relationships." He relied on their advice when he had to act promptly and the circumstances made it difficult to develop a thorough, thought-out plan of attack.

There are many other qualities that contributed to his professional success other than strong mentors and a sound career plan. Howie's persistence, dedication, eagerness to learn and passion all served him well from day one as an intern in the organization. His eagerness to learn helped him develop a relationship with Tom Heckert to gain experience in personnel matters and enhance his ability to evaluate talent. As he was able to display this knowledge, he continued to learn from Joe Banner and Andy Reid.

Howie's career and his advice in this chapter reinforces the importance of a career plan to obtain a specific position in the sports industry. For aspiring general managers, he advises you to identify your most likely route into the operations side of an organization and accept the first position that is offered. He also encourages you to think of ways to expand your knowledge in the area of your interest while surpassing the expectations of management in the areas for which you are directly responsible. This is paramount. Otherwise, you may not be with the organization for long.

10

EXECUTIVE DIRECTOR OF A PLAYERS UNION: THE PLAYERS' VOICE

DeMaurice Smith – Executive Director for the National Football League Players Association.

"Manage your emotions and keep everything between a three and a seven to make the best decision when presented with complex, high-profile issues."

DeMaurice Smith went from never working in sports to being named Executive Director of the most powerful players union in all of professional sports in March of 2009. In doing so, his story dispelled the notion that you have to work directly in sports for years to obtain an executive level position in the industry.

I met with DeMaurice and his Assistant Executive Director of External Affairs, George Atallah, in Washington, D.C., to familiarize myself with the responsibilities of the NFLPA and gain a better understanding of DeMaurice's role as Executive Director of one of the largest player unions in professional sports.

The NFLPA is the labor organization tasked with representing NFL players during the collective bargaining negotiations with the NFL and in many different aspects of their careers. DeMaurice never envisioned leading the NFLPA, but after two terms as Executive Director, he was re-elected for a third term in March of 2015 and will be up for re-election in March of 2018, just before the expiration of the NFL's Collective Bargaining Agreement.

*   *   *   *

As a graduate student from the University of Virginia's School of Law, DeMaurice started his legal career with a small boutique firm that focused on white-collar crime. This led to an opportunity with the U.S. Attorney's Office in 1991. He focused on violent crimes in the homicide section before joining the transnational terrorism section.

DeMaurice was preparing and trying cases at the highest level early in his legal career. He tried criminals that committed atrocious acts. This taught him the importance of managing his emotions in high pressure, crucial situations. In the late 1990's, he received an offer to serve as counsel for the U.S. Deputy Attorney General, Eric Holder.

These experiences equipped DeMaurice with the relationships and litigation experience sought by larger firms. He left the public sector and was hired as a partner with the international law firm Latham & Watkins in 2001. He represented some of the top corporations and these corporations' executives in the areas of white-collar crime and other litigation matters.

DeMaurice served in this role for seven years when he took his practice with him to Patton Boggs, a large law and lobbyist firm founded by Tom Boggs. He also sat on the transition team for the then-current senator in Illinois, Barrack Obama. He was preparing to be the U.S. Attorney in the District of Columbia if the presidential election unfolded the way that he believed it would.

Everything changed when he received a phone call from a search committee on behalf of the NFLPA in November of 2008. The NFLPA was conducting a search to find a replacement for its previous Executive Director, Gene Upshaw, who had served in that role for 26 years before his sudden passing on August 20, 2008. The search committee identified roughly 300 individuals that would be considered as his replacement. This list included non-traditional candidates with outside business experience, as well as sports industry executives in various roles, including sports agents, sports attorneys and past presidents of the NFLPA.

DeMaurice was intrigued by the call. He knew very little about sports business. But he did some initial research on the purpose of the NFLPA and the status of the NFL. His research revealed the likely opt-out of the then-current Collective Bargaining Agreement by NFL owners. He also identified a significant increase in revenue streams across the NFL accompanied with an uptick in litigation, both from former players and interested third parties.

These factors all suggested to DeMaurice that what the NFLPA needed was a leader to fill the void created by Upshaw's passing. "The players on the executive committee had an Executive Director that had the job longer than some of them had been alive, which is a very important frame to view this situation." He believed his litigation experience and leadership abilities qualified him for this role. The initial screenings and interviews went well, and the number of candidates was reduced to 25. At that point, he decided to remove himself from consideration for U.S. Attorney for the District of Columbia and went all-in for a chance to become the next Executive Director of the NFLPA.

He committed himself to understanding the NFLPA in its entirety. He assembled a team to dissect the organization and identify the different business functionalities of each department. DeMaurice and his close group of advisors also analyzed the legal complexities that impacted the NFLPA's relationship with the NFL and its 32 member-owners. This analysis included a breakdown of the three antitrust exemptions passed by Congress that extend to the League's operations, stadium funding mechanisms, the labor rights of the Union and the difference between a lockout and a strike (and more importantly why this mattered).

What started as initial research evolved into a 250+ page "Playbook" that set forth his strategic vision and tactical approach to the upcoming collective bargaining negotiations that would likely occur following the 2010 NFL season. This became his running platform.

After roughly 60 days of planning, DeMaurice met with the executive committee for the first time in November of 2008. The message he repeatedly delivered to them was, "This has little to do with the person you pick and more to do with the plan you pick." He also reiterated that the players' stake in the NFL's operations represented a $4 billion business. He impressed the executive committee and advanced to the final round of interviews.

The executive committee selected four candidates to speak in front of all 32 player representatives in March of 2009. These candidates included DeMaurice Smith, David Cornwell, Troy Vincent and Trace Armstrong. David Cornwell was a prominent sports attorney and veteran in the industry, while Troy Vincent and Trace Armstrong were former NFL Players Association presidents.

DeMaurice addressed the player representatives and highlighted his plan for the Union. He covered his strategic approach to the upcoming negotiations and explained how his background representing top executives for some of the world's largest companies would benefit the Union. He wrapped up his presentation and prepared for his departure from the hotel when he was informed that he needed to leave his cell phone and return to his room while the players submitted their votes.

At that point, the only thing he could do was wait. He ordered room service and kicked his shoes off. He finished his meal and was awakened by a loud bang on the door. He answered a bit groggy and was surprised to see Kevin Mawae, who was the President of the executive committee. He told DeMaurice, "You are our new leader."

De recalled walking into the office his first day and thinking to himself, "How am I going to take over a staff of 120+ employees without knowing a single one and make this whole thing work?" He began by working with outside consultants and conducting a more elaborate assessment of the entire organization: communications, public relations, salary cap, legal, marketing and the executive leadership team. They determined what worked, what didn't work, where the immediate risk existed and the best strategy to deal with it all.

For example, the NFLPA was sued by former players and a judgment was awarded in the amount of $20 million. The NFLPA could have pushed for a retrial, but that would have adverse consequences given that the goal was unifying the players for the upcoming collective bargaining negotiations. A strategic decision was made to settle the award at a lower amount outside the public's eye and shift all the attention to the players' wellbeing, both former and current, moving forward.

DeMaurice was also at a disadvantage because the previous executive director was deceased. He really didn't have anyone to consult that could offer a historical perspective on the organization. So he turned to executive directors in the other professional sports leagues. Shortly after he was elected Executive Director of the NFLPA, he had dinner with Marvin Miller and Michael Weiner, two former executive directors of the MLBPA.

They reiterated the importance of getting the players' buy-in right out of the gate and remaining visible along the way. DeMaurice knew that it would be impossible to make every player happy, so he focused on the high profile players that controlled their respective locker rooms. Marvin and Michael also advised him, "Despite what they say, the owners never want an outcome that is truly fair for both parties. There is always something greater at stake for them."

He visited all 32 organizations twice during the 2009 calendar year in furtherance of his player unification efforts. This was important because he was the new guy and he had to gain the trust of the Union members that he now represented. "They had to be aware that a 'war' was on the horizon."

He also met with the different stakeholders and learned which relationships were key and which relationships he could do without. This included understanding the different players in the media and using them to deliver a consistent message on behalf of the NFLPA. DeMaurice identified three main constituents that he needed to reach and had a specific message for each constituent.

These constituents and the corresponding messages delivered to the media were as follows: (1) Fans – the deliberate use of "lockout" and avoidance of "strike" and "work stoppage" to emphasize that this was the owners' decision; (2) Players – the deliberate use of the term "war" in reference to previous comments made in the media; and (3) NFL – the deliberate use of language to dismiss the presumption that both sides would get along because Gene Upshaw and Paul Tagliabue, the former NFL Commissioner, always did.

In addition to the use of strong rhetoric in the media, DeMaurice had to identify the key issues the NFLPA would focus on during the negotiations. First and foremost, it was very likely that the owners would demand a significant reduction to the players' share of revenues. It was also likely that ownership would look for new ways to increase revenues, which could include a proposed 18-game season.

He was aware that the NFL had a $4 billion reserve account funded by guaranteed television revenues, which could be used to indemnify the 32 owners if the 2011 NFL season was lost. In comparison, the NFLPA had $200 million to weather the storm. This put the NFLPA at a significant disadvantage, so DeMaurice's first course of action was to place the parties on a level playing field. This meant challenging the availability of the $4 billion in television revenues in the event of a lockout.

This challenge eventually made it to U.S. District Judge David Doty, who declared that the NFL violated its agreement with the Union. The Union sought an injunction, which would remove these television revenues from what the media coined the NFL's "war chest." To increase the protection of its players, the NFLPA purchased an insurance policy that would guarantee each player a six-figure salary if the season were lost.

After this ruling, the Union focused on its strategy with respect to the various issues and educating players and other stakeholders of the Union's positions. A key teaching point was the impact a single percentage point reduction in revenues would have on the players' salaries, the severity of which increased based on the length of the agreement. "A 15% decrease in player revenues would result in an annual loss of $600 million at the NFL's current revenues, which are certain to go up. Even if revenues remained stagnant, you would give up $3 billion if the parties agree to a five year term. That is unacceptable."

DeMaurice also focused on player safety. He addressed the looming concussion issues and the lack of healthcare for former players. This concern was exacerbated by the League's desire to expand to an 18-game schedule, which was a non-starter for the Union. Not only would the anticipated increase in revenues be insufficient, but the health risk to players made an 18-game schedule even more difficult to comprehend.

DeMaurice acknowledged, "The average career for an NFL player is 3.2 years. It takes three credited seasons before a player's long-term healthcare benefits vest.[xvi] Increasing the number of games will increase player injuries and could decrease the average career span to below three years, which would have a detrimental effect on players across the board."

The collective bargaining agreement negotiations played out, and eventually a deal was struck on July 25, 2011, without losing any of the 2011 NFL regular season. The 2011 CBA will expire following the 2020 season.

Ten years of labor peace meant that DeMaurice could shift his focus to all of the other responsibilities he had as Executive Director. His first priority was educating the players on their rights, benefits and responsibilities under the CBA. He has done this by visiting all 32 clubs and meeting with each club's players annually starting in August and wrapping up in November.

De attends the NFLPA Collegiate Bowl every January to connect with the NFL prospects that are invited to showcase their skills in front of the 32 clubs. He connects with another class of high caliber NFL prospects at the NFL Combine every February. In between these events, he makes an appearance at the Pro Bowl and Super Bowl. The annual player representative meeting is held every March, followed by the executive committee meetings leading up to the NFL Draft. He attends the Rookie Premier to help rookies acclimate to life in the NFL.

He also focused on creating services for members of the Union to maximize the benefits made available to them. They developed the Trust, a program designed to assist former and current players in the areas of post-career, medical, nutrition and education services. He established a wellness team in conjunction with the Trust to assist players and improve their lives. These services included drug rehabilitation services, professional transition assistance geared towards life in the NFL and education assistance for players that left college without a degree.

Then you have your everyday player issues. DeMaurice was very involved in the high-profile player discipline matters, including those involving Ray Rice, Adrian Peterson and Greg Hardy. The NFLPA took the NFL before an independent arbitrator alleging that roughly $120 million was wrongfully excluded from football revenues. The independent arbitrator ruled in favor of the players, finding that the $120 million stemmed from ticket revenues over the past three seasons that were improperly excluded under the NFL's CBA. The result is roughly $50 million back in the players' share.

Since he took office, the NFL's popularity has skyrocketed and League revenues climbed from $8 billion in 2009 to a reported $13 billion in 2015. Owners and players are getting richer, but the outlook of professional football isn't all positive.

A class of more than 4,500 former players agreed to a $765 million settlement over concussion-related brain trauma and injuries related to their involvement in professional football. The greater concern that received the majority of the media's attention was the notion that the League agreed to the settlement to protect from disclosure internal files that may have confirmed the League's knowledge of the dangers of concussions. Concussions led to numerous early retirement decisions in the 2014 and 2015 seasons and continue to jeopardize the future of the NFL.

Similar to the League, not all the reports are positive on DeMaurice's performance as Executive Director. Opponents of his routinely criticize the outcome of the 2011 CBA negotiations. One particular area is the amount of power the Commissioner has with respect to player discipline. This came to light in Deflategate, the title given to Tom Brady's suspension for his alleged deflation of footballs in the 2014 NFL playoffs. Another area of criticism relates to players' salaries and the reduction in rookie contracts. The NFLPA quickly points out that the top picks in the Draft saw their salaries reduced under the 2011 CBA, but the rookie class as a whole saw an increase in their salaries.

DeMaurice was faced with eight challengers when he was up for re-election in March of 2015. After running unopposed for re-election in 2012, his challengers took advantage of the player discipline issues that surfaced in 2014 in an attempt to force him out. After a round a presentations from each candidate and smaller breakout discussions, the player reps re-elected DeMaurice for another three-year term. He will serve as Executive Director through February of 2018, when the players will decide whether he will lead them in the next round of negotiations against the NFL owners following the 2020 season.

*   *   *   *

Q & A: DeMaurice Smith's Advice on Becoming an Executive Director for a Players Association

Q. Name the top three qualities that an executive director of a players' union must possess?

A. Understanding all of the risks and the complexities of the issues and managing your way to the most right decision.

Q. As executive director, what areas do you have to be knowledgeable in to be successful?

A. You have to understand the corresponding sports league just as well, if not better, than you understand your organization. Franchise owners are superior businessmen/businesswomen that look to expose weaknesses and capture revenue opportunities, so you almost need to step into their roles with that mentality to truly protect the Union's members.

Q. For aspiring executive directors, how do you recommend they gain the experience or understanding necessary to one day be named your successor?

A. Find a way to learn the myriad of issues that are really at play in the business and understand how the role of a labor union must fit in that paradigm.

Q. If you were to hire someone to be your successor, what are the skill sets that are required?

A. Someone that understands game strategy and relentlessly considers the potential outcomes for every decision.

Q. As executive director, what do you expect of every single person that is employed by the NFLPA?

A. Perform at a very high level and minimize the number of mistakes you make in your role.

Q. What is your best piece of networking advice?

A. Have friends the day before you need them.. – Tom Boggs

Q. Who are the top 5 most influential people in your career/network?

A. (1) Tom Boggs (Lobbyist and Founder of Patton Boggs) – he was a very successful national lobbyist that taught me about game strategy and how it all fits together. He knew what was really going on behind the scenes. He was not only brilliant, he did a great job teaching me how things worked v. how they appeared to work.

(2) Eric Holder (82nd United States Attorney General) – he taught me how to balance family against a job that can easily consume you.

(3) Ed Garvey (former Executive Director for the NFLPA) – his combination of intelligence and humor is unlike anyone else. He was the first Executive Director of the NFLPA.

(4) Marvin Miller (former Executive Director for the MLBPA) – he taught me what this position was truly about and that despite what everybody will say, especially the League, it is never truly "just business" and there is no such thing as a fair resolution across the board. He eventually endorsed DeMaurice in the New York Times as the right person for the job.

(5) Mike Weiner (former Executive Director for the MLBPA) – he was a fantastic mentor and the only contemporary person that I could speak to about the position. He taught me the importance of getting the key players on board and to buy into your vision. He was the most generous indulger of my chronic stupidity.

Q. What is the best piece of professional advice you received during your career?

A. Family first. This is something I've learned. I've had four jobs that I was convinced would be my last job. At the end of the day, the joy a family brings to your face far exceeds the feeling of professional success.

Q. What has been the biggest challenge during your tenure as executive director of the NFLPA?

A. Complicated problems with imperfect solutions are the most challenging part of this job. The media is always willing and able to criticize the outcome of every decision.

*   *   *   *

When DeMaurice received a call from the search firm tasked with organizing a candidate pool of potential successors for Executive Director of the NFLPA, he was intrigued. His intrigue turned to significant interest after a few months of planning and preparation. DeMaurice identified the importance of keeping your emotions between a three and a seven, but the greater takeaway is what it takes to do this successfully. It takes planning and preparation.

For those aspiring to become executive director of a players union, one major skill set to exhibit is thorough game strategy during the planning process. This role is public facing. DeMaurice will tell you that is the worst part of the job. Every decision impacts multiple stakeholders, both internal and external. He must consider every potential outcome and prepare a plan for how to respond to the actual outcome in every situation.

He emphasized the extent to which they would talk game strategy. If X, then Y. If Y, then either A or B, etc. This eliminates surprises and makes for the most efficient, accurate plan of attack. While De picked this up from Tom Boggs, he acknowledged that this is something he does ad nauseam.

The role of executive director of a players union also demands a delicate balance between management responsibilities and substantive work. As an elected official, DeMaurice serves on a limited term (three years) and must be re-elected to continue serving in this role. He must get buy-in from the well-known, influential players. This required not only being in front of the players, but also accomplishing change and making additional services available to the union members. This balance must be achieved at all times to succeed in this role and gain re-election.

DeMaurice Smith is the only contributor in this book that transitioned careers later in life with zero experience working in sports before doing so. Alec Scheiner transitioned from a law firm to the Cowboys, but the majority of his work at the law firm was sports related.

He identified the necessary skill sets and professional experiences to succeed in the role of executive director of a players union before he decided to pursue the position. He possessed these skill sets and professional abilities through his work as an attorney in both the public sector and private sector. The transferability of these skill sets helped him convince the 32 player representatives that he was the right man for the job.

DeMaurice's path into the industry suggests that you don't always have to start at the bottom or make peanuts for years to obtain an executive-level position in the industry. However, to do this successfully, you need to identify the transferrable skill sets that are required to succeed in the desired role. The same transferrable skill sets that led to his emergence as Executive Director, e.g. litigation experience, strong negotiator, game strategy, etc., will likely support his candidacy when he is up for re-election in 2018, just before the highly anticipated expiration of the NFL's CBA in 2020.

11

SPORTS AGENT: THE ART OF MANAGING HIGH PROFILE ATHLETES

Jim Steiner – former NFL Certified Agent

"This business is about relationships. If you know how to treat people and service your clients with honesty, integrity and the right morals, you will eventually succeed."

Jim Steiner represented between 300 and 400 professional athletes in his 35-year career as a sports agent. His client list included Hall of Fame players and other notable athletes like Jerry Rice, Michael Dean Perry, William Anthony Perry "The Fridge", Trent Green, and Shaun Alexander. Not bad for an aspiring stockbroker that happened to become a sports agent.

The athlete representation business has evolved significantly over the past 35 years. The strengthening of player unions, implementation of the salary cap and escalation of player salaries created a market for attorneys, entrepreneurs and other professionals to assist athletes and manage their affairs. The changes that took place from 1976 to 2012 introduced new players into the business and emerging circles of influence for professional athletes, including agents.

In 2015, it was reported by the National Football League Players Association (NFLPA) that roughly 813 individuals were certified as sports agents. The NFL allows 53 men on each club's active roster, for a total of 1,696 players. This number fluctuates during the season with injured reserve players and other player designations that don't count towards the active roster limit, but at the start of every NFL season, that's a ratio of roughly 2.08 players to every 1 agent.

This level of competition has significantly altered the way sports agents do business today. I met Jim for dinner at a small brewery in Ferguson, Missouri. Jim's success as an agent is remarkable and certainly worth covering for aspiring agents, but I also wanted to highlight the rejection that is certain to occur and capture his advice on what it will take to succeed as a sports agent in such a saturated industry.

*   *   *   *

After graduating from USC, Jim planned to stay in L.A. in search of a position with a brokerage firm. This changed when his father passed away in 1976, so Jim returned to Saint Louis to work in his father's business, which distributed electronic components across the country.

Jim wasn't fond of the industry, but it was something to engage in until the next opportunity surfaced. He was responsible for wrapping up his father's business affairs, which eventually resulted in his father's partner exercising his right to buy Jim's family's stock in the business.

Around that same time, Jim's uncle introduced him to Richie Bry. Richie was getting ready to open a sports agency in town with the support of an influential professional baseball player, Lou Brock. Lou played in the major leagues for 18 years, ending with his retirement in 1979. Lou was a 6x All-Star, 2x World Series champion, 8x National League stolen base leader and the father of Richie's son's little league teammate.

In 1977, Richie hired Jim to help with the launch of Bry & Associates. His starting salary in 1977 was $7,000.

They started from scratch. Lou offered to spread the word regarding their new agency, and he referred both Garry Templeton and John Denny, intriguing minor league prospects with huge upside who Richie and Jim felt could be big time major league players. They both became clients.

They did everything for these two minor leaguers, which included marketing services, financial planning, contract negotiations and anything else they requested. Garry Templeton experienced instant success in the major leagues, notching All-Star selections in two of his first three seasons. John Denny was a 6'3", right-handed pitcher drafted by the Saint Louis Cardinals in the 1970 amateur draft. He made his rookie début for the Cardinals in 1974.

The success of their first two clients helped with the agency's marketability. Lou continued to refer prospects, and Richie and Jim found themselves representing a lot of the Saint Louis Cardinals' roster.

The agency was growing. They identified that they could fill a similar niche by representing players in the National Football League. Richie continued to grow the baseball business, while Jim shifted his focus to professional football in 1978.

At the time, the NCAA didn't regulate a collegiate player's amateur status and state regulations had yet to surface. Cash was being thrown around by agents without any regulation to prevent it. Sure, it may have been perceived as unethical, but it wasn't illegal.

In his first season recruiting, Jim was able to secure in-person meetings with Earl Campbell, the legendary running back and Heisman candidate, and Raymond Clayborn, a high caliber cornerback, both from the University of Texas.

He flew to Austin, Texas, and met Earl Campbell after the Oklahoma v. Texas rivalry game. Earl was sitting in his dorm room after the game and his lip appeared very swollen. Jim led with, "Geez Earl, what happened to your lip?" It was chewing tobacco. Needless to say, he did not sign Earl Campbell. The next day, he met Raymond in his dorm room. He never left the comfort of his bed, so Jim pitched Raymond bedside. The bed sheet never slipped below Raymond's nose. He knew he wasn't going to sign either prospect.

He left Austin discouraged. He seriously questioned whether this business was for him. "I was a 24-year old with zero experience representing professional football players. I felt I had no business being there, but the desire remained."

But he kept on plugging away. He built strong relationships with prospects and established a connection with their family members and friends that would influence their decisions. Leading up to the 1979 Draft, he made great progress with potential first round picks Dan Hampton, a big defensive end out of the University of Arkansas, and Kellen Winslow, a tight end out of the University of Missouri and an East Saint Louis native.

Jim was convinced he was going to sign Dan and Kellen, but he quickly learned how difficult the sports agency business could be. Dan Hampton signed with Michael Trope, a leading sports agent at the time. But his disappointment transitioned to excitement when he learned that Kellen Winslow wanted to sign with Bry and Associates. His relationships with members of Missouri's coaching staff were pivotal in positioning him to sign Kellen following the 1978 college football season. Early in his career, Jim had a potential first round draft pick as a client.

As they prepared for the 1979 Draft, Jim received word that Dan wasn't happy with his current agent and wanted to switch representation. Dan did what he had to do on his end to get himself out of his contract with Trope. Once he did, he immediately signed with Jim as the Draft was fast approaching.

He continued to build strong relationships with his clients as they prepared for the NFL Draft and finished school. The business was different in 1979. Training facilities did not exist and teams rarely spoke with agents prior to the contract negotiations discussions. They waited patiently to see where they would be playing football that season. There was very little to do other than focus on building strong relationships.

The Chicago Bears drafted Dan Hampton in the first round, fourth overall, in the 1979 NFL Draft. Kellen Winslow went off the draft board shortly thereafter. He was selected as the 13th pick in the 1979 NFL Draft by the San Diego Chargers.

Jim learned a lot about the business through his interactions during the pre-Draft process with the Chicago Bears' General Manager Jim Finks. He was a class act, and Jim admired the way he handled the negotiations with him. Where other general managers may have tried to strong arm a younger agent with such a high profile client, Jim Finks approached the negotiations in a relaxed manner, akin to that of a partnership trying to come to an agreement.

The year 1979 proved to be a pivotal one in Jim's career. He had two players selected in the first round of the same NFL Draft class. His success positioned him to ink multiple players in the early 1980's. Some of these prospects included Howard Richards (26th pick, 1981 Draft), Jeff Griffin (61st pick, 1981 Draft), Don Greco (72nd pick, 1981 Draft) and Mike Pagel (84th pick, 1982 Draft).

Jim made a name for himself in the business and across campuses, primarily in the Midwest. He hit these schools hard during the recruitment process, and his efforts were rewarded. In 1983, Jim signed Roger Craig, a running back out of the University of Nebraska, and Dave Rimington, the two-time Outland Trophy winner and center for the Nebraska Cornhuskers.

Dave Rimington was drafted in the first round of the 1983 NFL Draft by the Cincinnati Bengals with the 25th pick, and Roger Craig went 24 picks later with the 49th pick to the San Francisco 49ers.

Jim continued to sign big name prospects on the football side. In 1985, he added William Anthony Perry "The Fridge", a defensive tackle out of Clemson. He also landed Randall Cunningham, quarterback at UNLV and projected top quarterback in the 1985 class. They were selected 22nd and 37th respectively in the 1985 NFL Draft.

With so many high-powered clients that were happy with his services, Jim started to receive veteran referrals. He recalled receiving a call from Roger Craig. Roger said, "I have a client for you." He excitedly asked, "Who?" Roger's response, "Jerry Rice."

Jerry Rice was a first round pick in the 1985 NFL Draft by the San Francisco 49ers that had a promising first season in the Bay area. He netted 49 catches for 927 yards in his rookie season and all signs suggested that a very successful career was in store for him.

Heading into his second season, Jerry was unhappy with his agent. Jim immediately booked a flight to San Francisco and spent hours with Jerry and his wife to get their finances in line. They were so pleased with him and the financial plan he put together for them that Jerry signed with him.

Jim started to get the itch to start his own agency. He acknowledged, "Richie was responsible for my initial success in the industry. He gave me my first opportunity." However, Jim started to question his future with the agency and believed it was time to go out on his own. He approached Richie about purchasing the football division.

Richie was open to selling and secured an accountant and an attorney to value the business. They determined that the value of the client list and the corresponding future revenue streams was $100,000. This was a substantial amount of money in 1987, but Jim knew the business and considered it significantly undervalued. A deal was struck and Sports Management Group was formed.

He was ready to roll. The only problem was the NFL players weren't. In 1987, the National Football League Players Association went on strike and replacement players were utilized. With a new house, two kids, and a $100,000 loan in repayment, he wasn't sure how long he could last if his clients weren't earning an income that would generate his fees.

Luckily his concerns didn't last long. The majority of players returned after week four, which weakened the Union's position and ultimately led to the end of the strike early in the 1987 season.

He remained focused on recruiting a strong class for the 1988 Draft: the first class on his own. He signed Eric Moore, a highly coveted prospect that played tackle for Indiana University. He also signed Michael Dean Perry, a defensive tackle out of Clemson. Eric and Michael went 10th and 50th overall in the 1988 Draft.

Jim continued to experience success with his clients in the NFL Draft, but he was also signing free agent prospects and veteran players that dropped their agents. From 1989 – 1992, he added nine players through the NFL Draft.

He utilized interns to help him service his existing clients and research to identify future prospects. He would receive phone calls from various high school and college students looking for an opportunity. One such phone call came from Ben Dogra. Ben was a student at Saint Louis University that was willing to do the work for free.

Ben knew nothing about the business, but Jim liked his passion and persistence. Ben was offered an internship with Sports

Management Group. When Ben first started, he was tasked with creating brochures and other administrative tasks. Jim recalled taking Ben on a recruiting trip months after he became an intern. They failed to sign the big name prospect, and he took this hard. But Jim saw potential in Ben and identified that he had a knack for the business. In 1992, he hired Ben full time.

The two of them became a dynamic team. They worked the phones early and often. As they worked together, they got better and better. If they got in front of a prospect for a final interview, typically they signed him. From 1993 to 2000, they signed various clients, including Trent Green, Mike Alstott, Mike Flanagan, Jon Runyan, Warrick Dunn and Chris Chambers.

As the business continued to experience change, so did the responsibility of sports agents. The Collective Bargaining Agreement (CBA) established the players' rights with respect to medical treatment, healthcare and other professional benefits. The CBA also governed player fines, grievance procedures and appeal rights. Agents became responsible for helping their clients understand these areas and assisting with filing injury grievances, non-injury grievances, injury settlements, fine appeals and requests for second medical opinions.

Around this same time, the athlete representation industry experienced a shift. Large entertainment corporations began acquiring smaller agencies with an added appeal to athletes, opportunities in entertainment. The Assante Corporation acquired the firm Steinberg, Moorad & Dunn, a leading sports agency. [xvii] International Management Group, better known as IMG, represented athletes and entertainers around the globe. Jim was aware of this change in the industry, so he wasn't surprised when he was approached by SFX.

SFX Sports and Entertainment was a publicly traded company led by entrepreneur and entertainment executive Robert Sillerman. SFX acquired many different sports agencies representing athletes in the Big Four, highlighted by its acquisition of David Falk's agency, F.A.M.E, in 1998. [xviii] Falk was most well known for his representation of Michael Jordan and Patrick Ewing, among other NBA superstars.

SFX wanted Jim's client list, which at that time consisted of 60+ professional football players. He would receive a large sum of cash in exchange for essentially his client list and the perks of self-employment. As part of the deal, he would become an employee of SFX under contract for six years and would lead SFX's football division. Jim looked at the upfront cash he would receive as part of the deal, as well as the yearly compensation and incentives which, if hit, would equate to what he was accustom to earning. He viewed this as an opportunity to make 10-12 years of income with one swoop of the pen.

In April of 2000, they agreed to terms. SFX acquired Sports Management Group.

At the time of the acquisition, professional football's revenues surpassed those of professional baseball and professional basketball around the year 2000. And since the players' salaries were, and currently are, tied to the League's revenues, this resulted in an increase in player salaries. An agent's true payday came with a client's second contract, which typically occurred four-to-five seasons after a player's rookie season.

With over 25 years of experience negotiating NFL contracts, Jim was in a great position to use his expertise to secure the biggest deals for his clients. In 2000, Jon Runyan signed a six-year, $24.5 million contract with the Philadelphia Eagles. He then negotiated a six-year, $22 million contract for Mike Alstott. In 2001, Jim inked a five-year, $11 million deal for his client Mike Flanagan.

Endorsement opportunities for players surfaced with the popularity of professional football. Agents were tasked with locating these local and national marketing opportunities, which included autograph signings, radio show recordings, product endorsements and personal appearances. SFX was in a great position to tap this market and attract top talent based on its entertainment presence and relationships.

As head of SFX Football, Jim set his expectations high for the 2001 NFL Draft. Virginia Tech's quarterback, Michael Vick, was the most elusive, multi-faceted weapon of the class and experts projected him to be the first overall pick.

Jim and Ben made progress with the Vick family over the course of the 2000 college football season. They positioned SFX as one of the favorites to land Vick and were invited to meet with Michael and his family following his final season. They knew that it was imperative that the Vick family understood and trusted that Ben Dogra and Jim Steiner were on the same level and that his needs would be handled by a great team at SFX.

Taking this one step further, they decided to have David Falk attend. David was the head of SFX's basketball group and Michael Jordan's agent. They took a private jet to Virginia to meet with Mike Vick. Jim's instructions to David on the plane were simple, "We need your support as an executive of the company with ties to the greatest professional athlete of all time, but, when it comes to representation and football matters, Ben and I will handle everything."

The meeting started off well. They talked about the plan they had for Mike and the services that SFX could offer. One key piece of their proposal was the marketing exposure the company had access to via Michael Jordan and other high profile clientele. They acknowledged that Vick's endorsement potential was enormous, and they had the relationships and resources to capitalize on this. David Falk covered everything he was asked to, but he didn't stop with the endorsement pitch. He went on and told the Vick family that, "I'm the head of SFX, Jim is the head of SFX Football and will negotiate your deal, and Ben is Jim's assistant." They did not sign Michael Vick.

He may have missed on Vick, but he didn't miss on others in the 2001 Draft. He signed Justin Smith, a highly-touted defensive end from the University of Missouri, located right in Jim's backyard. He continued expanding his geographic reach, signing Deuce McAllister, running back out of the University of Mississippi; Matt Light, tackle for the Boilermakers of Purdue; and Torrance Marshall, linebacker from Oklahoma University.

Justin Smith was drafted 4th overall by the Cincinnati Bengals. Deuce McAllister went 23rd to the New Orleans Saints, Matt Light was selected by the New England Patriots with the 48th pick and Torrance Marshall went to the Green Bay Packers with the 72nd pick overall.

They continued to add clients via the NFL draft, but they also retained clients due to the value they brought to the contract negotiations. Ben and Jim secured a six-year, $32.5 million contract for wide receiver Chris Chambers. Jim negotiated a three-year, $19 million dollar deal for Warrick Dunn, running back with the Atlanta Falcons. Trent Green signed a three-year extension (seven years total) with the Kansas City Chiefs for a total value of $51 million

Ben continued to evolve as an agent and establish himself as a force to be reckoned with. The two of them signed clients like Bryant McKinnie (7th pick, 2002 Draft), Jeff Faine (21st pick, 2003 Draft), Roy Williams (7th pick, 2004 Draft), Lee Evans (13th pick, 2004 Draft), Vernon Carey (19th pick, 2004 Draft) and Jake Grove (45th pick, 2004 Draft).

In 2006, they recruited many prospects, none more promising than Mario Williams, a defensive end out of North Carolina State. It was obvious that Mario would be a high first round pick, but an agent's job is to get his high 1st round client to be the 1st overall pick.

Teams dedicate unthinkable resources to vetting players and gathering information on NFL prospects. They knew that a few other prospects were being considered in that first slot. Reggie Bush posed the greatest threat. The two jockeyed for positions, but as the 2006 Draft approached, Jim's and Ben's experience shone through. They were willing to establish the parameters of the deal if Houston selected Mario first, whereas the inexperience of Bush's agent made him hesitant to do so.

Mario Williams was drafted #1 by the Houston Texans.

Despite the success of SFX Football and the other divisions, a large merger led to its exit from the sports market in its entirety. Each former owner still controlled the players/clients in their respective sports that could leave at any minute, so valuing the business for a single transaction proved difficult. Instead, everyone ended up buying their positions back from SFX for roughly 25 cents on the dollar.

Creative Artists Agency (CAA) was one of the most dominant entertainment agencies in the world at the time SFX exited the business. CAA wanted to buy Jim and Ben's business, and, ultimately there was a three-way transaction between CAA, SFX and Sports Management Group.

Following the cash transfer, Jim and Ben signed 6-year contracts with CAA in 2006, joining super-agent Tom Condon and others as part of the CAA team. When he signed the deal, he felt he had six more good years to give. The team of certified NFL agents at CAA worked well together and accomplished great success following the acquisition.

In the first three seasons together, CAA netted 20 first round draft picks. These clients included Jake Long and Matthew Stafford, who went #1 in their respective NFL Draft classes. This level of success in the industry launched CAA to the top sports agency and hushed critics that speculated such a combination of sports agents (presumed to have big egos) couldn't be successful. A star-studded client list and access to Hollywood through its entertainment division helped ensure the company's continued success.

The escalation of rookies' and players' salaries that the industry experienced in the early 2000s continued into the latter part of the decade. In comparison, the first overall pick in the 2000 NFL Draft received a reported seven-year, $35 million rookie deal, while the first overall pick of the 2009 NFL Draft agreed to a reported six-year, $72 million rookie contract.

Jim and Ben's clients that they signed prior to joining CAA headed into free agency as unrestricted free agents. Bryant McKinnie signed an eight-year, $30 million deal with the Minnesota Vikings. Ben secured a five-year, $35 million contract for wide receiver Lee Evans with the Buffalo Bills. In 2009, Jim negotiated a six year, $45 million contract for client Justin Smith. These are just a few examples of the lucrative deals Jim secured for his clients.

Jim was an integral part of the company's initial success, but as his contract was approaching its final year, he was ready for his next challenge. The 2011 NFL Draft was his 34th NFL Draft as a sports agent. He left CAA after the expiration of his employment contract and began pursuing a career as a financial advisor at the end of 2012.

Jim navigated the agency business as an inexperienced agent, an owner of an agency and an executive of the largest sports agency in the industry. He experienced player strikes, the formation of the players' union and the economic dominance of the NFL that led to a significant increase in players' compensation. He also represented multiple first overall picks, and, through all of his experiences, he identified what it takes to succeed as an NFL agent in an incredibly competitive field.

*   *   *   *

Q & A: Jim Steiner's Advice on Becoming and Succeeding as a Certified NFL Agent

Q. Name the top three qualities that a sports agent must possess?

A. You must be able to relate well with others and associate with all walks of life. You must have fantastic communication skills – articulate with a commanding presence. And you must have thick skin with a very short memory.

Q. As a sports agent, what other areas of the business do you need to be knowledgeable in?

A. Everyone reads about contract negotiations and player compensation. This is a big component of being an agent, but you also must be knowledgeable in the NFL's Collective Bargaining Agreement, including the salary cap, grievance procedures, appeals process, medical rights, etc. You will also need an eye for talent and an understanding of the X's and O's, unless you have someone that can take care of that aspect of the business for you.

Q. How has the industry changed since you started in the business?

A. As the players' compensation continues to grow, the competitive nature of recruiting will make the business even more difficult to succeed in. This along with the compensation formula for rookies makes it very difficult for smaller agencies to recruit and eventually sign promising prospects.

Q. For aspiring professionals, how do you recommend they gain the experience necessary to one day become an NFL agent?

A. Do whatever you can to get in with an established agency and learn the business, whether it is as an intern or a full-time employee. Starting your own agency from scratch is very difficult and almost impossible given today's environment.

Q. Name one person that helped you break into the industry.

A. Richie Bry – I credit Richie for all the success I had as a sports agent. He opened doors for me in the industry that taught me the business. He helped me understand what it would take to succeed as an NFL agent.

Q. What is your best piece of career advice?

A. Keep your nose clean, be committed to your craft and treat people honestly and fairly. Position yourself to work for the right people that are going to give you an opportunity to advance the ball. This may take a couple different stops. In order to get there, have something that you do, a specific skill, so that you can tell them what makes you better than other candidates. Never say, "I want to be an agent because I like sports"...that will get you an escort to the front door."

Q. How do you recommend approaching and networking with sports agents to position one's self for future opportunities?

A. Do some research on the top firms and ask the gatekeeper who the right person is to speak with regarding the best way to obtain a position at those firms. Ask questions like who does the hiring, who screens applicants and who is the best contact person? You should also call the Players Association and get the agent directory for a complete list of registered agents to identify the top agencies in the country.

Q. Who are the top 5 most influential people in your career/network?

A. (1) Richie Bry – He is responsible for my emergence as a sports agent.

(2) Jim Finks – Jim was the general manager of the Chicago Bears when they drafted my client Dan Hampton. He helped Jim with his approach to the NFL clubs and how to best position his clients for the NFL Draft.

(3) Jim Turner – Jim worked on the baseball side with Bry & Associates, and we stayed together in an unofficial capacity until 2000 when SFX acquired my agency. We worked through a lot together and both became better businessmen through these experiences.

(4) Ben Dogra – Ben was my best hire and having him as a part of my team was a big benefit for me. The way he learned the business, mastered the art of recruiting and managed his clients' careers was very impressive.

(5) My wife, Pat – Without her patience and understanding, I would never have been able to succeed. Being an agent is a 24/7

proposition and if you are married with kids, you better have your priorities in order.

Q. What is the best piece of professional advice you received during your career?

A. It's all about the people you associate yourself with when it comes to managing your business. Finding the people that have the same values and ethics as you do.

Q. What would you tell someone that gets a late start in the industry, but aspires to be a sports agent?

A. If you are over 50 – forget it. If you are over 40, don't do it. You have a slim chance of successfully entering the business and succeeding. If you are in your 30s, approach the business with an understanding that it will take you 5-10 before you start to see a monetary return. You must find a way to support your way of life (i.e., kids, wife, school, bills, etc.) while you make a name for yourself in the industry.

Q. What was the biggest challenge during your time as an NFL agent?

A. The biggest challenge was the recruiting component. It was competitive and not for the faint of heart.

*   *   *   *

During our interview, Jim offered praise for my path into the industry and what I had accomplished up until that point, but my presence in front of him didn't impact his advice to aspiring agents, which was quite simply, "Don't do it!" I informed him, "This is a career how-to book. I'm not sure that advice will work!"

He laughed, and we started to talk about the business based on our very different experiences as sports agents. While the athlete representation field has changed drastically since Jim first started as an agent in 1977, the fundamentals of the business have, for the most part, remained the same.

Relationships are key, but the right relationships are often overlooked. The relationships that most young agents incorrectly focus on occur on the front end (i.e., potential clients, prospect family members, etc.). Of course these relationships are very important, but the relationships that will lead to a sustainable sports practice are on the back end (i.e., NFL scouts, general managers, reporters, trainers, etc.). Jim identified Jim Finks as one of the most influential persons in his career, and this is why. Jim helped him understand how to approach teams, how to market his clients and how to position his clients for success in the NFL. The advice that stems from these relationships is far more impactful than the advice you will ever receive on one particular prospect.

He also advises that one of the three most important skill sets or personal characteristics to have in this business is the ability to relate to others. Sports agents are more closely scrutinized now than ever before. As an agent, you can't provide anything of value, which includes promising something of value in the future as an incentive to become a client. The ethical agents that do this are at a disadvantage, so the only option is to win over a prospect during phone conversations and/or the final meeting with a prospect after his eligibility has expired.

These phone conversations and meetings are often very quick. You have a limited window of time to impress, so it is important that you can relate and establish a good rapport. It is not uncommon to meet in an apartment, a fast food restaurant or a prospect's family room. The socio-economic status of prospects ranges from the richest of the rich to the poorest of the poor. It is important that you become comfortable with the uncomfortable.

Lastly, Jim recommends entering the business gradually or with an established agency. Here are the realities. Training costs are very expensive. Prospects demand these services, and most of them require a facility in Florida. These facilities range in cost from $10,000 - $75,000, depending upon the circumstances. Marketing guarantees have become somewhat of the norm and are absolutely necessary to sign a high-end prospect. Prospects might also expect massages, transportation, weekly stipends, merchandise and personal attention. It is a very costly process.

An agent's primary way to recoup these expenses is through an agent's fee permitted by the NFLPA, which is capped at 3% of a player's earnings under his contract. The Collective Bargaining Agreement negotiations in 2011 simplified the player contract negotiations process. This made it possible for prospects to demand a lower percentage, which they now often do. The simplification of player contracts for drafted prospects included a significant redistribution in compensation, with almost every player drafted outside of the second round making the league minimum paragraph 5 salary.[xix] This earnings redistribution is illustrated by comparing Sam Bradford's contract and Cam Newton's deal, both of whom were drafted with the first overall position of their respective draft class, 2010 and 2011.

My point to all of this is that profit margins are shrinking, which makes it more difficult to enter the sports agency business as your only source of income. Going back to Jim's advice, "You won't start to make money until 5-10 years in to your career." For the most part, this is true, so you need to be very strategic with how you decide to enter the industry.

And the current agent environment supports this position as well. It is estimated that 42% of certified agents do not have an active client in the NFL, 25% of agents have between one and four clients and 25% of the certified agents represent roughly 78% of the active players in the NFL.[xx] The sports agency business has numerous barriers to entry, so these statistics aren't that surprising once you learn more about the business.

Jim hit the nail on the head when he said, "*If you know how to treat people and service your clients with honesty, integrity and the right morals, you will **eventually** succeed.*" I chose to emphasize the word **eventually**. It will take you time to develop the right relationships, sign clients, service clients and, most importantly, retain clients. You will be fired. You will experience setbacks. But if you continue to work hard and do all the things necessary to be a successful sports agent, you will eventually succeed. Just don't expect it to be over night.

12

SPORTS PSYCHOLOGY: THE MENTAL ASPECT OF THE GAME

Jason Selk – former Director of Sports Psychology for the Saint Louis Cardinals

"No matter what field you are in, you better have a value proposition, something that you are clearly better at than everyone else that will in some way contribute to the business making more money."

The great Yogi Berra once said, "Baseball is 90% mental. The other half is physical." If sport is really more mental than physical, why did it take so long for organizations to focus on the mental aspect of the game? The Saint Louis Cardinals hired Jason Selk in 2006 as Director of Sports Psychology. He was tasked with improving mental toughness, which, in theory, would enhance player performance on the field. That season, the Saint Louis Cardinals went on to win the 2006 World Series. He would remain with the Cardinals for six more seasons, culminating with the 2011 World Series Championship.

I first heard about Jason from a personal friend. He recommended that I reach out to him and learn more about his work with the Cardinals and his approach to accomplishing mental toughness. He not only led the Cardinals' mental training program from 2006 - 2011, but he is also a best-selling author and executive coach for sports and business professionals alike. He developed and provided a service that few others could offer, and the success he experienced in St. Louis and, subsequently in various industries, support that his approach works.

*   *   *   *

It took a serious knee injury for Jason Selk to realize his career interest was psychology. As a high school athlete undergoing significant physical rehabilitation, he found himself intrigued by the entire process. The idea of helping people and, more specifically, rehabilitating athletes appealed to him at first. While he began exploring this field, it dawned on him that he wasn't in love with the physical rehabilitation process. What captured his attention was the mental aspect of rehabilitation, the psychological component of healing and becoming better.

He decided to pursue this practice. He received his degree in Sports Psychology from the University of Missouri. Shortly thereafter, he attended graduate school at the University of Missouri-Saint Louis with a focus on sports psychology and the development of the human mind. He started to recall everything he learned in school and considered whether there was an existing, easy and operationalized scientific process for developing the mind to achieve greatness. His opinion was that there wasn't.

The creation of Jason's mental toughness regimen started on his back deck in 1999. He sat down with a pencil in hand and started writing down everything that came to mind. The goal was to develop a mental training program that met three specific criteria: (1) It had to be simple, (2) It had to be science-based and (3) It had to produce measurable results.

To be simple, he envisioned a program that could be performed in less than ten minutes. That was his duration threshold. He also wanted a program that would be easy to follow and commit to memory.

He was preparing for his oral exams in his doctorate program while simultaneously developing this plan, so he was equipped with all the information he needed to make sure his plan was science-based. He designed his mental toughness program equipped with the knowledge that the human mind can be trained to expel negative thoughts and activities that naturally occur. Negativity is counter-productive to high performance, so coaching your mind on how to handle such negativity optimizes performance. He focused on the core principles of sports psychology, which included the appropriate amounts of visualization and repetition. Jason finished writing out his plan in its entirety on scratch paper in less than an hour and his instincts told him that it would produce results for athletes.

He was ready to start testing his mental toughness program. Lucky for him, he was able to experiment on a friend that played professional baseball for the Houston Astros. He had his friend on the phone 15 minutes after he finalized his program, and his friend agreed to test his plan.

Jason acknowledged that he was incredibly fortunate to have a friend in the MLB that was willing to test his mental toughness routine. Otherwise, he would've had to start at the bottom with college and minor league athletes. It could have taken years to convince professional baseball players that his program would work at the highest level of competition.

His mental toughness principles produced results almost immediately. His friend was in the middle of a slump, reaching base only three times in his previous 30 plate appearances. He consistently performed these mental preparation exercises in Jason's plan and committed himself to the program. He achieved three consecutive weeks with 10+ hits as a result. This single professional baseball player became a believer and proven success at the professional level was all it took for his mental toughness approach to attract the attention of other athletes.

His success with his friend resonated with other athletes. He had roughly 15-18 fairly big named professional baseball players ask to be taught his program. His reach wasn't confined to Major League Baseball. He received calls from athletes in the NFL, NBA and NHL, among other professional sports leagues.

And not only did individual athletes seek out his services, but professional clubs took notice. His client list grew, and as it grew, players on different MLB clubs started asking their respective team's physicians and medical staffs questions about mental toughness programs. One person that fielded these questions was the Saint

Louis Cardinals' head physician. He called Jason in 2005 and asked him if he had any interest in meeting to discuss his training program.

In addition to serving as the Cardinals' head physician, he was also a consultant for all of Major League Baseball in matters related to drug and alcohol. Jason assumed that he was looking for his assistance with the development of a drug and alcohol rehabilitation program. Instead, Jason was informed that the St. Louis Cardinals' were interested in hiring him as Director of Sports Psychology.

He entertained the possibility of joining the Cardinals' staff and subsequently met with the Cardinals' General Manager, Walt Jocketty, to discuss the position. Walt expected tangible results. It was clear from day one that he would have to perform immediately, or else he wouldn't be around to teach mental toughness to the Saint Louis Cardinals. In return, exclusivity would not be a part of his contract. He would be free to work elsewhere so long as he met the required 20 hours per week.

Jason Selk accepted the Cardinals' offer and became their Director of Sports Psychology for an initial term of one year.

The MLB union prevented the organization from requiring that players work with him, but many of them wanted to work with him thanks to his reputation in the industry from his established clients. Of these players that rolled into his office, Jason recalled numerous players that committed to consistently performing his mental exercises. These players that consistently applied these principles saw improvement to their performance on the field. Those that inconsistently applied his principles did not experience this same increase in performance, which provided a strong basis for his presence in the clubhouse.

In his first season with the Cardinals, they went on to defeat the Detroit Tigers in the 2006 World Series.

He didn't track team statistics because not all of the players worked with him. The Cardinals' statistics don't clearly establish that his involvement in the clubhouse resulted in the organization's success, but a closer look at the individual players did. Scott Spiezio was one such athlete that experienced a career resurgence thanks to Jason's program. Scott recorded his second best batting average of his career and reached base on 112 of his 321 plate appearances in 2006.

Jason continued to emphasize that his clients needed to focus on the process of success and what it took to reach their goals, not the desired result. Each client was tasked with satisfying a simple 90% test: 90% on top of performing mental workouts before every practice or game, 90% success logs after every practice or game, and 90% on what Jason calls Relentless Solution Focus (RSF). According to Jason, "The athletes that do this, the proof is in the pudding. My thriving practice is a testament of this."

He relied on the momentum from his program's success with the Cardinals during the 2006, 2007 and 2008 seasons to go mainstream with his mental toughness routine. He put his mental toughness program in literary form, and his book *10-Minute Toughness* was published in 2008.

The Cardinals' owners were businessmen, and their satisfaction with Jason's performance in the clubhouse was made known to other businessmen in industries outside of professional sports. In 2009, he started receiving numerous requests from corporations and other businesses to work with their sales professionals and high-level executives on mental toughness. Jason began testing his mental toughness principles in industries other than sports.

He continued to work closely with the Cardinals' players. The number of athletes that chose to work with him increased. These athletes that committed to his program continued to see an increase in production and experience better performance in clutch situations. These were the results that Walt Jocketty demanded when Jason first joined the Cardinals, so he remained with the organization.

Entering the 2011 season, the Cardinals were five seasons removed from their last World Series Championships. The Cardinals needed to win, as the previous season resulted in one playoff appearance and fewer games won. The Saint Louis Cardinals went on to defeat the Texas Rangers in the 2011 World Series, marking the second championship during Jason's tenure with the organization.

In addition to his success in the Cardinals' locker room, he received more and more requests from professionals outside the sports industry. These requests, combined with his work in the clubhouse, made it difficult for him to do both. After the 2011 season, he stepped down as Director of Sports Psychology for the Saint Louis Cardinals to pursue these other business opportunities.

Whether his program was the primary reason for the club's success is up for debate. There were a number of factors that could have explained the Cardinals' success during the 2006 and 2011 seasons. But the fact that his arrival marked the first title since 1982 and his departure year marked the last title won by the Cardinals supported his mental toughness program as one of the key contributing factors.

His program helped professional athletes perform better in some of the most high-pressured circumstances and scenarios. His second book, *Executive Toughness*, was published in 2011 and focused more on traditional business roles (e.g. sales professionals, executives, officers, etc.). According to Jason, "Mental toughness applies to anyone that is motivated to improve and willing to do the work to get there."

He has gone on to assist professionals in many different markets. He has established himself as one the premier executive coaches and the leading sports/business psychologists in the country. Jason travels the country to speak at various corporate retreats. He inspires others to become better in their respective roles, and through his program, most of them do.

*   *   *   *

Q & A: Jason Selk's Advice on Maximizing Opportunities in the Sports Industry

Q. How has the industry changed since you started in the business?

A. Social Media, which amplified change within the teams. This constant exposure to the media and different fan bases forced teams to adjust and secure social media experts as early as 2009.

Q. Name one person that helped you break into the industry?

A. John Wooden and the lessons he taught. He did a lot in teaching people that sports are a vehicle to becoming a huge success or a great person, not that sports cause you to become a great person. His approach in focusing on process instead of results, while showing class and integrity the entire time, is remarkable.

Q. Your best piece of networking advice?

A. Identify something that you are better at than anyone else and pursue that area of expertise. You need to be top dog in that one thing you do and that thing needs to contribute to the business making more money.

Q. Who are the most influential people in your career/network?

A. (1) Walt Jocketty – To this day he is still the most genuine guy I have ever met in professional sports, and he helped me identify what I should focus on. He advised me to never ask players for favors, because doing so can sour the relationship very quickly.

(2) Tom Bartow – His uncle, Gene Bartow, took over for Coach Wooden at UCLA. Tom had a real background in sports and coaching, but he went on to become one of the most successful advisors at Edward Jones. He guided me into what I am doing now, which is coaching individuals, and Tom understands athletes, so he allowed him to keep his sports mentality on the forefront while working towards the business side.

Q. What is the best piece of professional advice you received during your career?

A. Two pieces of advice stick out, so I can't just name one.

(1) My father always told me that, "If you are going to do something, do it right." This took a long time to internalize, but I finally did.

(2) Coach Wooden would emphasize that true success is defined with effort and not results. "The best way to reduce results is to focus on what causes the result, as opposed to the actual result."

Q. What advice do you have for someone looking to create a position in the sports industry?

A. Every year sport becomes more and more specialized, so make sure you do one thing great. You must identify that one thing and establish proven results before sports teams will hurry to create a position for you.

Q. What is your most memorable moment in the sports industry?

A. Three come to mind: (1) winning the 2006 World Series and the realization of peace and relief at the thought of what this could do for my career, (2) working for 2008 USA Men's Gymnastics team that had no business on the medal stand but they took 3rd, and (3) *helping an 11-year-old gymnast win state and being the first person she called.*

Q. What is the one thing that every employer looks for in hiring an employee?

A. Work ethic has been so compromised, and there isn't a way to make it at the professional level without having a tremendous work ethic.

    *   *   *   *

Jason's path into the industry is very unique and, for that reason, difficult to emulate. He identified a need across sports organizations and then filled it. And while some of the professional sports franchises had already attempted to address this need, Jason was the first to create a mental toughness training plan that was simple, tangible and measurable.

He identified his passion at a young age and focused his studies and committed his personal time to understanding the human mind and crafting a plan that would accomplish mental toughness. I'm paraphrasing, but according to Jason, professionals need to identify what they do better than anyone else that increases the organization's bottom line.

He encourages readers to do this in his book, but he also instructs his clients and readers of his books to do the same. Similarly, I provide step-by-step instructions on how to perform an effective self-assessment in Part Three. Your likelihood of success in a particular role is so much greater where strong performance in a given position requires skills that align with your strengths.

He also focused on advice that he received from Coach Wooden, which was, "The best way to reduce results is to focus on what causes the result, as opposed to the actual result." This concept was instrumental in the development of Jason's mental toughness program, which focuses on the creation of process and product goals. Essentially, Jason instructs professionals to focus on what they need to do to accomplish their goal (process goals), as opposed to focusing on the overall goal (product goal).

For readers aspiring to work in the sports industry, the focus during the development of your networking plan and career plan should be on the steps you need to take along the way to ultimately obtain a particular role in the business. Similarly, the relationships you form during this process should be with industry professionals that will help you meet these different milestones in pursuit of your career goal.

Accomplishing a career objective, such as becoming a general manager or chief executive officer in professional sports, is a daunting task. It can take years to accomplish such a lofty goal, so it is important to focus on the steps that will get you there. If you ignore the daily/weekly/monthly activities that will help you acquire the knowledge necessary to achieve the larger objective, then it will be very difficult to obtain your overall goal. I refer to a similar approach for achieving your goals and ultimate career objective(s) in Part Three.

As you identify your greatest strength(s) later in this book, do so keeping in mind that you also must understand how your answer to this question will benefit the organization or company from whom you seek employment. Focus on the steps you need to take in order to accomplish your overall objective. In doing so, you will accomplish smaller, more manageable goals that collectively will result in the achievement of your overall objective.

13

INTERNSHIPS: THE NFL'S MOST STORIED INTERNSHIP PROGRAM

Charley Casserly – former General Manager for the Washington Redskins and Houston Texans

"You need to chase opportunity, not a title."

Charley Casserly's career in professional sports began as an unpaid intern with the Washington Redskins in 1977. He went on to climb the ranks in the industry and serve as General Manager for the Washington Redskins (1989-1999) and the expansion franchise Houston Texans (2000 – 2006). Unpaid internships can, and frequently do, serve as the initial step towards success in one's professional career.

As a product of the internship route, Charley remained committed to the program that existed in Washington until 1978, and, in 1983, he reinstituted the very program that contributed to his emergence in the National Football League. This internship program, which was originally started by George Allen, lasted 22 years under Charley's tutelage and heralds more than 30 professionals currently working in the sports industry. This decision resulted in one of the industry's most successful internship programs.

*   *   *   *

In April 1977, Charley convinced himself that a quicker route to becoming a Division I college coach was to gain experience working in the NFL and not to continue on the path he was on for the previous six years as a high school and college football coach at the lower divisions. He finished writing his letter, placed it in an envelope and sealed it. The recipient of his first letter inquiring about opportunities with NFL organizations was George Allen, Head Coach for the Washington Redskins. The other 27 NFL teams would receive a similar letter.

He eventually heard from 22 of the 28 teams. While most of the responses were discouraging, two clubs expressed interest in interviewing him for an unpaid internship. Those two teams were the Washington Redskins and the New England Patriots.

Charley's first interview was with the Washington Redskins' player personnel director Tim Temerario. Tim's claim to fame was helping Woody Hayes break into coaching as his graduate assistant. Five minutes into the interview as his nerves started to wear off, Tim jumped up and told him to go on to the next interviewer. Tim exclaimed, "Five minutes; I can analyze anyone in the world. Go to the next guy."

So he did. He went through a total of three interviews before he met with George Allen. George was known for his efficiency, and Charley's interview with him proved why. It began in a hallway and proceeded into the Redskins' coaches' locker room. Charley found himself shouting over the stall door in the bathroom at one point. This was bizarre, but he rolled with it. He wanted to make sure that Coach Allen understood he was serious about this opportunity, whatever it may be.

Coach Allen exited the stall and instructed him to spend some time by himself writing out three ways that he could help the Washington Redskins. Charley was warned by Tim and others on the staff not to write about coaching. According to Tim, "Coach Allen doesn't trust anyone under the age of 35 as a coach."

So Charley, uncertain of what exactly to say, began writing. He identified three ways he could help the Redskins: assistance in the scouting department, administration and anything else that needed done around the organization.

Coach Allen returned hours later and called him into his office. He read what Charley had written, but it wasn't enough to convince him to hire him. Coach Allen told him, "Go home and rewrite how you would help the Redskins, what you haven't done and what you would like to do in football, and what you would change in the NFL." He later learned that these were the three questions that George asked of every internship candidate.

He returned home and started writing. He spent more time on this response than he did on any of his assignments in undergraduate or graduate school. He focused on similar areas in his initial response, but elaborated upon how he would contribute to the scouting department and the organization. Despite his desire to become a coach, he never mentioned it in his response. He sent his response a few days later. That same day, he received a call from the New England Patriots. They wanted to interview him.

He was on his way to New England to meet with Head Coach Chuck Fairbanks and his staff. He interviewed with Coach Fairbanks, and the two discussed Charley's professional interests and why he wanted a position with the Patriots. Chuck never made eye contact, so it was difficult to tell if anything was resonating with him. Charley explained that his ultimate goal was to become a coach. At that point in the interview, Chuck called his defensive coordinator and other members of his staff into the interview room.

Chuck said to them, "Charley may intern for us, and he wants to coach in college. I'm not going to bring him in unless you swear to help him get a coaching position at the college level." Every coach in the room agreed. He finished the interview and went back home. A week or so later, he had a note in his mailbox at school. This note read, "Chuck Fairbanks called."

He immediately called Chuck Fairbanks' secretary and scheduled a call with Chuck on the next day at 11:30. He dialed George Allen's number and told George's secretary that he needed to speak with George at 10:15 regarding the opportunity with Washington. George called Charley and explained to him that everyone liked him, and they would like to offer him the unpaid internship. He thanked George but also informed him that before he accepted this position, he wanted to speak with Chuck Fairbanks in New England.

In retrospect, Charley acknowledges that he probably wouldn't have handled the situation in this manner. He spoke with Chuck, who offered him a mini-camp internship with the Patriots in June. When he mentioned that the Redskins offered him a full season internship that he intended to accept, Chuck wished him well. Charley called George Allen and informed him that he was looking forward to working for him in Washington. Charley accepted Washington's offer.

Through all of this, the one thing that stuck in Charley's head was something Coach Allen had said during his interview, which was, "I am looking for a person like me 26 years ago. Someone to open the place up in the morning and close it up at night." This philosophy aligned with his work ethic. At the time, he had $500 in the bank, 120,000 miles on his car and limited personal belongings due to an apartment fire that destroyed most of his belongings two years prior to this offer. He literally had nothing. His perception at the time was that he had nothing to lose.

He prepared to report in June of 1977, which included getting his financial situation in order. He would continue to receive paychecks through the summer months from his current employer, which he would save and use during the regular season. He also asked seven different family members and friends to loan him $500 each if he desperately needed it, which they agreed to do. Despite this financial safety blanket, he questioned his decision and whether he could endure an entire season without a paycheck.

Charley awoke in a cold sweat on his broken mattress situated in his apartment two weeks before he was set to report. He reminded himself that to do something great, sometimes you have to take chances. He stayed his course, and he now advises others that when making a decision of this magnitude, "You will have doubt, but you need to develop a plan and fight through this doubt to make it."

Charley reported to Washington's facility in June of 1977.

He went to work every day with Coach Allen's advice on his mind. As the only intern, his responsibilities included answering the camp telephones, doing daily tasks for the PR department, notifying players that they had been cut, driving players and personnel to the airport, breaking down film, preparing cut ups, scouting for the college and pro personnel departments and performing other tasks as assigned.

His first personnel assignment, which was communicated to him via a note on his desk, was to evaluate the Green Bay Packers. He didn't receive any other direction or advice. So he researched report formats and relied on his knowledge of the game acquired during his years of coaching at the high school level. He spent a lot of time on this assignment. It was his first opportunity to impress Coach Allen.

He was pleased with Charley's work. Charley performed these tasks up until the regular season, at which point he was transitioned to the scouting department under the internship program.

Since this was an unpaid, season-long internship, performing services as a scout meant that his travel expenses, meals and lodging were covered. He was on the road quite a bit evaluating college prospects for the next NFL Draft. When he came back to Washington, the team would put their scouts up in a hotel. He did this for the entire season until December, when he was called back to the Redskins' facility.

Charley spent most of December sleeping on a couch in an apartment with fourth round draft pick Duncan McColl, previous intern Charlie Taylor and undrafted rookie Mark Murphy (who is now the Packers' President and CEO). He continued to work unpaid up until the Washington Redskins chose not to re-sign George Allen in January of 1978. The Redskins' management approached Charley with a full-time job offer to stay with the organization in the scouting department. After seven months as an unpaid intern, he accepted the position with a base salary of $17,000.

He remained a true believer in internships that offer the same exposure and experience as a full-time employee. His support of the internship program was a product of his success as an intern under George Allen and the advice he received from his little league football coach and mentor, George McElwreath. Charley offered George $100 of his first reimbursement check with the Redskins as a sign of his appreciation of George, which he initially refused to accept. Instead, George told him, "If you think I helped you, then your job is to go help somebody else."

Charley climbed the ranks in the organization, and in 1983, just five years after he was hired full time, he was responsible for running the Redskins' training camp operations. He brought back the internship program with the intention of offering the participants a meaningful experience. He had this philosophy in mind when he contacted an administrator at the University of Massachusetts for a recommendation. The resulting recommendation was a young graduate assistant for Massachusetts' football program by the name of Steve Spagnuolo.

Charley decided to meet with Steve and interview him in a hotel lobby on his way to scout players at Boston College. He recalled Steve doing a nice job in his interview of expressing his desire and communicating his experience. Based on his interview and a strong recommendation, he hired Steve as his first intern in the summer of 1983.

The intern program started out with two spots. Personnel would house one intern while the other intern focused more on public relations and communications. Charley's intern would help prepare for training camp, create cut ups, chart plays during practices, evaluate players, document practice activities and assist with the administration of training camp. He would retain interns for more than one internship period if they did not land a full-time position following the internship, but his preference was to make this opportunity available to as many different aspiring professionals as possible.

This internship program continued and even expanded as he climbed the ranks in the organization. Charley was promoted to General Manager of the Washington Redskins in 1989. He held this role for 10 seasons and maintained the program until his departure from Washington in 1999.

When the Houston Texans made Charley the General Manager of the expansion franchise, he implemented his internship program in 2002. One drastic change to the internship program in Houston was that he would no longer retain an intern for more than one internship

*   *   *   *

Charley's footprint is all over the National Football League. Despite not hiring interns since his departure from the Texans in 2006, his program heralds 30+ former interns still active in professional and collegiate athletics. These former interns occupy positions in scouting departments, salary cap departments and various departments on the business side. These individuals are located in every geographic region in the country. His program has produced three general managers in three different professional sports leagues: Mike Maccagnan (New York Jets), Billy Eppler (Los Angeles Angels) and Sam Hinkie (Philadelphia 76ers). The following list identifies these former interns.

Kevin Abrams – N.Y. Giants	*Michael LaFlamme – HOU Texans
Mike Maccagnan – N.Y. Jets	Eugene Armstrong - DEN Broncos
*Barry Asimos - HOU Texans	Steve Spagnuolo – N.Y. Giants
Tim Bald - St. Norbert College	Dave Emerick – Washington State
Dwaune Jones - BAL Ravens	Trip MacCracken – KC Chiefs
Mark Olson – DET Lions	Jamaal Stephenson – MIN Viking
Jeremy Breit – N.Y. Giants	Jedd Fisch – University of Michigan
Rob Kisiel - HOU Texans	Tom McGaughey – CAR Panthers
Monti Ossenfort – NE Patriots	Tricia Turley – Towson University
Scott Cohen – BAL Ravens	Joel Patten – CAR Panthers
Jean Paul Dardenne – NO Saints	Bill Dekraker – N.Y. Jets
Kevin Murphy – BUF Bills	Matt Winston - MIA Dolphins
Eric DeCosta - BAL Ravens	Brian Hudspeth – TB Buccaneers
Rob Lohman - DET Lions	Ian Nelson – Syracuse University
Dave Sears - DET Lions	Carter Chow – Yee/Dubin Sports
Dave Butz – Sports Stars	Sean Finucane – Converse
Billy Eppler – L.A. Angels	*Ray Wright – WAS Redskins
*Sam Hinkie – PHI 76ers	

* Indicates last place of employment

period. He did this for two reasons. First, similar to what Chuck Fairbanks promised to him during his interview, he felt an obligation to help his interns obtain full-time employment, even if this wasn't with his employer. The second reason was that he wanted to make sure that he made this initial opportunity available to as many aspiring professionals as possible.

Charley's oversight of the internship program came to an end on June 1, 2006, but the program continued after his departure. The success of Charley's program is proof that the internship route works. It's just a matter of finding the right internships, positioning yourself to be considered for those opportunities and making the most of the opportunity presented.

*   *   *   *

Q & A: Charley Casserly's Advice on Breaking into the Sports Industry

Q. If you could offer some advice to individuals breaking into the sports industry, what would it be?

A. Do a great job at what you do and please who you are working for, but learn other aspects of the business through osmosis and your own hard work. Don't wait for work. When you finish the work assigned, find another assignment or do something that will benefit the organization.

Q. What is the best piece of professional advice you received during your career?

A. Be the first one in and the last one out. And while you're at the office, ask yourself "Is what I'm doing now going to help the organization win?"

Q. Who are the top five most influential people in your career, excluding family, and why?

A. *(1) George McElwreath (little league football coach) – He told me, "If you think I helped you, then your job is to go help other young people." This resulted in the hiring of his first intern, Steve Spagnuolo, in 1983.*

(2) George Allen (former Head Coach for the Washington Redskins) – Coach Allen taught me to prioritize and become more efficient. Coach Allen had a sign on everyone's desk in the organization, "Is what you're doing now going to help us beat the Cowboys?" My motto became "Is what you're doing now going to help us win?"

(3) Joe Gibbs (former Head Coach for the Washington Redskins) – He taught me the importance of preparation. During his press conference announcing him as head coach of the Washington Redskins, he stated, "The single most important thing is to prepare for the job, because you only get one chance."

(4) Bobby Beathard (former General Manager for the Washington Redskins) – I learned a lot from his philosophy on evaluating talent and managing people during his tenure as GM of the Washington Redskins.

(5) Jack Kent Cooke (former Owner of the Washington Redskins) – His attention to detail and mental toughness are two attributes I took from him.

Q. When you look to hire someone, what is the most important quality or qualities you look for in an applicant?

A. *There are a few qualities I looked for when hiring interns: (1) work ethic – all the successful ones had great work ethic, (2) intelligence – the ability to anticipate work and think ahead to meet*

the team's needs, and (3) self-starter – the motivation to m[...] the industry and the drive to make the organization better.

Q. Any guidance with respect to how to secure a posi[...] the sports industry?

A. *When you apply for a position, apply to a s[...] department. Once you are there, they will teach you what you[...] to do and how to do it. Do everything as if you were doing it f[...] owner.*

Q. What is your best networking advice?

A. *Send a written thank you note regardless of your experie[...] or outcome with an organization, because people remember[...] written thank you note. There are very few ways to make a last[...] impression in the industry, and this is something that will reson[...] with most professionals.*

Q. What has changed the most since you entered the NFL?

A. *From a business perspective, growth i[...] marketing/advertising and advances in technology. Biggest change[...] to the game itself are the implementation of the salary cap and free[...] agency.*

Q. What is your most memorable moment as an employee in the industry?

A. *Winning the Super Bowl as General Manager for the Washington Redskins versus the Buffalo Bills in 1992.*

As I browsed this list, I recognized a large majority of them. I decided to solicit feedback from a few of them to help readers understand the value of an internship in the sports industry. These former interns included Steve Spagnuolo, Defensive Coordinator for the New York Giants and former Head Coach for the Saint Louis Rams; Eric DeCosta, Assistant General Manager for the Baltimore Ravens; and Mike Maccagnan, General Manager for the New York Jets.

Steve Spagnuolo: Charley's First Intern

Steve Spagnuolo has experienced it all on the coaching front. He was the head coach of the Saint Louis Rams from 2009 - 2011. He held various coaching positions with multiple clubs, including the Philadelphia Eagles, New York Giants and New Orleans Saints. Steve also coached across the pond, spending one season with the Frankfurt Galaxy as Defensive Coordinator.   Regardless of the position, Steve opined, "I can't think of one position that I have held that didn't trace back to Charley and his staff in Washington and/or to my experience as the first intern under his program in Washington."

Steve came highly recommended as a candidate for an internship in Washington. He was serving as a graduate assistant and football coach at the University of Massachusetts when they agreed to meet at a hotel nearby to get further acquainted. According to Steve, "I wasn't certain how many other candidates were being considered, but I quickly learned that Charley was too thorough to select someone based on a single recommendation." He relied on his knowledge of the game from his experience at Massachusetts to convince Charley that he was a worthy candidate.

In the summer of 1983, Steve became the first intern under the re-instituted program in Washington.

He had a great foundation of knowledge about the game and arrived at training camp bright-eyed and enthusiastic. One of his first assignments was to put together a drill book for the position coaches.

He conducted a lot of research to identify different drills he could include in this book. He recalled, "This was before the internet made this type of search relatively easy."

Steve was also responsible for compiling what Charley referred to as an internship diary that would document his experiences and responsibilities as an intern in Washington. He listed every job, regardless of how glamorous or mundane. His approach to the assignment was that if this were going to be shared for years to come, he intended to document everything.

The projects he worked on for Charley and the coaching staff provided a direct link to the staff. He surrounded himself with great coaches that understood he wanted to become a coach in the NFL. The quarterback's coach assigned Steve to chart passes, assist with QB drills and document the day's activities and results. Other coaches took notice of his involvement in position drills.

The offensive line coach of the legendary "Hogs" extended him an invitation into the offensive line film room. He took advantage of this. Word spread and soon Steve was invited into the team meetings led by Head Coach Joe Gibbs. He used this as an opportunity to take notes and learn everything he could about the strategy behind the game. That was until Coach Gibbs expressed concern in the amount of notes Steve was taking during the meeting. He recalled, "All head coaches are paranoid, and the amount of writing I did in my notebook during these meetings was initially a cause for concern." He made the wise decision to listen and learn during subsequent team meetings with Coach Gibbs.

His internship came to an end before the 1983 NFL regular season. He went on to coach football at various levels, culminating with his first opportunity as a head coach with the Saint Louis Rams in 2009. Steve credits his internship opportunity and the industry professionals he met in Washington for his success, stating, "Working for people that are willing to pick up the phone and serve as a reference is the key to being successful in this industry."

Eric DeCosta's Emergence in the National Football League

Eric DeCosta was a graduate assistant coaching football at Trinity College, a Division III program, when he started catching wind of personnel internship opportunities in the NFL. He enjoyed coaching and the perspective it gave him on the sport, but Eric already identified that his passion was around roster construction, salary cap and building a successful franchise from the ground up. Eric hoped to use his understanding of defensive and offensive schemes and the nuances of the game to make himself more marketable to NFL personnel departments. He started writing letters to every NFL team inquiring about an opportunity in personnel.

The Washington Redskins were the first and only organization to respond in the spring of 1995. Scott Cohen, who previously completed a training camp internship in Washington and was now full time with the organization, called Eric and informed him that they would like him to submit his information in consideration for a six week, unpaid training camp internship.

He submitted his information and was selected for the initial round of interviews. He did well enough in his first interview to advance to the second round of interviews. He learned that training camp would begin in mid-July and end in late August, which meant he could complete the internship, if offered, and return to Trinity College if he didn't receive a full-time job.

Eric underwent the second round of interviews, and it was expressly acknowledged that they appreciated his understanding of the game as a coach. He made it clear that he wanted the training camp internship because his true passion was scouting and personnel. Following the second round of interviews, the Redskins extended training camp internship offers to six individuals, one of whom was Eric DeCosta. He accepted immediately.

He was initially responsible for setting up and maintaining the players' dorms. This required him to install cable televisions, prepare the rooms and make sure the players had everything they needed during camp. This wasn't the type of work he expected to be doing, but he didn't let this prevent him from learning about player evaluations. He made himself available at the facility and absorbed information through his interactions with coaches and members of the personnel department.

Eric recalled "sitting around the office after standard work hours and listening to the coaching staff, specifically Cam Cameron, Norv Turner and Ray Horton, talk about the game." This is where he learned the most.

A few weeks before his internship was scheduled to end, Charley asked him to make cut ups of offensive and defensive lineman for him to review. Eric's primary advantage over the other interns was his coaching experience. This was his opportunity to display his knowledge of the game and prove to Charley directly what he could do.

He analyzed the film and selected the plays where the linemen in question exhibited skills and abilities that were necessary for success in Washington's scheme. His final work product displayed what he learned while coaching at Trinity and listening to the coaching staff around the Redskins' headquarters. Charley complimented Eric on this project and indicated that his abilities were apparent.

As training camp came to an end, Charley and Scott singled Eric out and told him that he did a great job and that they would help him get a full-time job in the NFL. Unfortunately, a job was not available with the Redskins. He returned to Trinity College following his internship.

Eric was considering pursuing a different career path after a year had passed since his experience in Washington when he received a call from Scott Pioli with the Baltimore Ravens. Scott Pioli informed him that Scott Cohen had recommended him for an entry-level personnel position. The applicant pool was very strong, and the Ravens ultimately had to choose between Eric DeCosta and

Les Snead. He was offered the position in the spring of 1996 and has spent the last 20 years with the organization. He was promoted to Assistant General Manager in 2012, a position he has held as of the publication of this book.

Looking back on his emergence into professional sports, Eric advised, "What makes internships so valuable and helps professionals move up in the business more than anything else is the connections you make and the mentors that you can reach out to that will help you learn more about the game."

He acknowledged, "We have a lot of people that want an internship with Baltimore and it is a lot more competitive. Students and young professionals have very little experience, so without football experience, it will be very difficult to get even an unpaid internship." He advises to volunteer at the local high school as a coach or work in the football office at a smaller college before searching for internships in the NFL. "Without this experience, you will not be a good candidate – the fact that you are in college or are young will not get you an internship anymore. You need experience."

Mike Maccagnan: Intern to General Manager

Mike Maccagnan was headed for Wall Street as an investment banker. He took a break from his employment search to attend his sister's college graduation ceremony at Dickinson College in Carlisle, Pennsylvania. Dickinson College had been hosting the Washington Redskins' training camp since the 1962 NFL season.

While on campus, he ran into Scott Cohen at a local function. Scott was a senior at Dickinson who served as the head scouting intern for the Washington Redskins after working two seasons as an intern under Charley's program.

They talked football and the NFL Draft, which was one of Mike's obsessions at the time. Though Mike didn't know a lot about operations/scouting/personnel at the professional level, Scott told him exactly what was expected of training camp interns and shared his experience on the personnel staff. He also informed Mike that he was responsible for hiring the other training camp interns and that one of the interns for the upcoming camp bowed out, creating a vacancy that needed to be filled. Scott indicated that the position was available if he were interested. Despite having to start at the very bottom, Mike was intrigued.

He shared this opportunity with his parents. They thought it was odd that he would want to serve as a training camp intern while searching for employment with an investment banking firm. Mike was confident that he could pursue this opportunity and complete the internship, if presented, before he would be done interviewing for jobs on Wall Street. He thought it would be a great way to spend the summer, so he expressed his interest to Scott and was subsequently offered this training camp internship with the Washington Redskins. He accepted in the summer of 1990.

Mike reported shortly thereafter with a decent idea of what to expect. It started with a lot of grunt work – dormitory prep, practice prep, player services, car rides, etc. The importance of the task didn't really matter to him. He was excited to be behind the scenes with an NFL team with access to the players and front office staff. He quickly learned that while not all jobs are newsworthy or carry significant importance, every job serves a greater function. According to Mike, "In an organization, everyone has a job to do, some small and others large. If each person does their job to the best of their ability, then the organization will succeed."

Under Charley's internship program, doing the little jobs well would lead to larger projects with exposure to Charley and his staff. Charley wasn't always accessible to his interns, but Mike recalls him going out of his way to make time for them when he could. Mike worked very long hours and would engage in casual conversations with team executives in between the tasks he was assigned. He maximized this time with them and would pick their brains about the industry to better position himself for a full-time opportunity when one presented itself.

Roughly a month into the internship, Mike was tasked with his first assignment that would illustrate what he learned during training camp and display his ability to evaluate talent. He was tasked with providing film cut-ups for Charley on players at different positions. These cut-ups consolidated film on a particular prospect, but that was the extent of the information. So Charley would solicit the creator's opinion on the prospect's ability and gather additional information on each prospect. When Charley asked Mike about the players for whom he provided cut-ups, he could tell that Mike understood talent and was a sound evaluator.

His internship was wrapping up when the Redskins' Director of Personnel received a call from Dan Rambo, who was a league scout for the World Football League. Dan was looking for talented scouts to join the World Football League. Charley wanted to keep Mike on staff, but they didn't have any opportunities at the time. The organization recommended him for the job, and he received an offer and moved overseas to work for the World League.

Mike would go on to work for the London Monarchs of the World Football League and the Ottawa Rough Riders and Saskatchewan Roughriders of the Canadian Football League, before returning to work for the Washington Redskins as a "combine scout" in 1994. In this role, Mike served as the team's representative to BLESTO, one of two scouting combines that pool its member clubs' resources to evaluate talent for the upcoming year's Draft. He served in this position for one year before being promoted to a hybrid college and pro scouting role.

Mike continued to advance on the personnel side. He remained with the Redskins until Charley was hired by the Houston Texans as General Manager, at which point he became Charley's first hire in Houston. He continued to refine his craft and enhance his knowledge on all matters related to the operations side of the business until he was ultimately named General Manager for the New York Jets in 2015.

Mike encourages younger professionals in the industry to remain focused on doing their job for the organization and to engage with high-level executives only when an opportunity to do so arises. He suggested, "Don't force these interactions. These managers/executives will acknowledge your hard work and, if you do your job properly, they will reward your effort with career advancement."

Finally, he discourages professional advancement via politicking. He believes that leading an organization requires understanding the business and the nuts and bolts of the organization, which uses many different experiences to capture. Those that advance via industry politics will have a greater chance of failure due to the complex nature of the business. According to Mike, "Professional sports is an unforgiving business, so the best way to ensure a long, successful career in the sports industry is to do your job to the best of your ability as you work your way up the ladder."

It isn't a coincidence that over 30 former interns for Charley Casserly remain in the industry. More often than not, the success or failure of an internship opportunity is the result of the intern's attitude, approach and performance. But the likelihood that an opportunity leads to full-time employment is greater when the position offered is under the control of professionals that acknowledge and appreciate this route into the industry.

Charley encourages aspiring sports professionals to look for internship opportunities that will equip the participant with the knowledge and skills necessary to secure full-time employment. The narratives that highlight these executives' experiences under Charley's tutelage support the premise that an unpaid internship can be the start of a very successful career in the sports industry. According to Eric and Steve, the connections made while serving as an unpaid intern can be just as important as learning about your specific area of interest. This is a difficult balance, so look to gain the respect of these individuals by working hard and displaying your willingness to do whatever it takes to help the organization while furthering your career and building your network.

The benefits of a quality internship are very apparent. And while not everything about internships is positive, it is possible to reduce the negative attributes by identifying the quality, established internship programs that are administered with the participant's career interests in mind. Opportunities exhibiting these qualities represent your greatest chance for success.

TIPS TO IDENTIFY QUALITY INTERNSHIPS

1. Research the career paths of executives in the organization. If they started with the organization, this is a strong indication that the organization develops within.

2. Find out whether the high-level executives started as an intern. If so, there is a greater likelihood that they will have an appreciation for this approach and reward the hard work of interns.

3. Rely on your network to obtain inside information about the internship. Why was it created? How many interns have they had in the last two years? Past five years?

4. Look for common points of origin for the different executives. An ex

---

PART TWO RECAP

The preceding chapters offer insight on how difficult it can be to obtain a specific position in the sports industry. Some of my contributors interned in multiple cities and in different areas of the business before finding their true niche. Career paths aside, every contributor offered something of value to the organization that aligned with his or her skill sets.

The professional advice offered by my contributors varies depending on the position and stage of the contributor's career. However, the majority of the tips provided in Part Two pertain to succeeding in a particular role. Thus, it will help you only after you obtain a position in the sports industry. In addition to this position-specific guidance, I started to identify career advice and recommended approaches into the industry that have general applicability. Keep in mind the following takeaways as you explore and eventually obtain a position in the industry.

1. **Become an expert in your area of the organization first and then focus on advancement.** While this comes off as common sense, it is something that is easily forgotten. People incorrectly believe that networking and forming relationships with various executives in the organization is a high priority from day one. I made this mistake. The reality is that management's satisfaction almost always precedes upward movement, unless you are the owner's son or family member. Fight the urge to over-network and focus on your job. If you do this, advancement opportunities will soon follow.

2. **Identify different ways to acquire a skill set that is currently lacking but necessary for future advancement.** The majority of my contributors discuss sitting around the headquarters or listening in on

conversations among other employees. A few examples include Steve Spagnuolo's time in the meeting rooms listening to the coaches, Kevin Abrams' tit-for-tat lessons on salary cap and personnel evaluations with the scouting department and Ethan Waugh's exposure to the advanced scouts while working as a scouting coordinator. It didn't take a formal opportunity for these contributors to learn more about an area of the business in which they lacked experience and/or knowledge. Look for these opportunities to establish a baseline knowledge in an area outside of your expertise and position yourself for advancement.

3.   **Evaluate opportunities based on experience offered and new skill sets to acquire, not title or money.** It is human nature to desire a powerful title or high salary, and you can still obtain your dream job in such a fashion. But some industries are different and your only option may be to take what is perceived as a step back to take two steps forward. Don't hesitate to do so if it is the right opportunity. Your network will help you make this determination.

4.   **Seek out a mentor.** Every contributor expressly acknowledged or alluded to the importance of a mentor. Howie Roseman cites Mike Tannenbaum and Ryan Grigson. Jim Steiner references Richie Bry. And Brian Gainor encourages others to focus on who they work for and not what they are responsible for when seeking a position in sports. When seeking a mentor, don't force these interactions. Instead, pay attention to which individuals in the organization offer to help and the employees that come highly regarded by other employees. A strong mentor can assist you in understanding the office politics and help you succeed in your present role.

**PART THREE: MY ASSESS, DEVELOP, IMPLEMENT
APPROACH TO NETWORKING AND YOUR
NETWORKING PLAN**

Every contributor in this book identified their interest in the industry and the position that would best fit their interest and skills. This recognition is very important. *The convergence of your skills and interests with a particular position is often where your greatest likelihood of success lies.*

I developed a networking approach that would put me in place to identify the best position for me right away and then pursue that area of the industry from day one. I determined what helped me connect with others. Most importantly, I relied on the advice of the members of my network to refine my approach. What resulted was my networking plan, which focused on building the right relationships in the industry that could help launch my career.

My networking plan – the same plan that helped me secure a position in an NFL front office and led to my emergence and success as an NFL agent - is comprised of three stages:

(1)   **ASSESS** – Gain an understanding of your strengths, weaknesses and professional interests, which serves as the foundation of your networking plan.

(2)   **DEVELOP** – Create your networking plan by identifying the professionals that are in a position to help you succeed and developing content that will facilitate conversations with these individuals.

(3)   **IMPLEMENT** – Build your network and connect with industry executives who will enhance your knowledge in a particular area and help you land the position that you desire.

14

ASSESS: SELF-AWARENESS THROUGH SELF-REFLECTION

I began mentoring and speaking with students and young professionals in 2012 following my experience in the 49ers' front office and emergence as an NFL agent. It immediately became apparent to me that most people aspiring to work in sports lack clarity around what it means to work in sports. But another shortfall I've identified through my interactions with these individuals is a lack of self-awareness.

This lack of self-awareness is most prevalent in young professionals and students. They have limited experience in a corporate setting and minimal exposure to business relationships that help identify one's strengths and weaknesses. While this is typically outside the person's control, inadequate self-awareness is also the product of limited self-reflection, which is entirely within the person's control.

My different experiences in the industry brought to light my strengths and my weaknesses. More importantly, my exposure to the industry confirmed my passions. This helped me develop my own approach towards an effective self-assessment, which is laid out for you below.

Step One: Identify your strengths and weaknesses through self-reflection.

An accurate self-assessment begins with identifying 7-10 strengths and weaknesses through self-reflection. While obtaining this number is important, it is the manner in which you perform this self-reflection that has the greatest impact on the success of this exercise.

It should be performed without the assistance of others. In fact, limiting external influences is paramount. One person's opinions can cast doubt on your perceptions of what you do best and the areas in which you struggle, as well as call into question your professional goals and career aspirations. You will eventually solicit feedback from others. However, now is not the time.

It is also important to focus on your strengths and complete this list before moving on to your weaknesses. Narrowing in on your weaknesses first could distort your awareness of your strengths and skew the results. But this does not mean that you neglect your weaknesses. As a senior level executive and talent recruiter for a Fortune 100 company advised me, "Failing to acknowledge your weaknesses could derail the progress made by understanding your strengths."

Begin your self-assessment by focusing on your strengths. Once you open yourself up to honest self-reflection, attributes and skill sets start to roll off the tongue. After you identify where you excel, do the same for your weaknesses. You will develop a level of comfort in discussing your weaknesses and identifying areas for improvement. Strive to identify seven to ten in each category. My initial list should be used as an example to help you come up with responses on the next page.

Strengths Assessment

MY STRENGTHS	YOUR STRENGTHS
• relate well	• _____
• creativity	• _____
• business acumen	• _____
• risk taker	• _____
• determined	• _____
• idea generator	• _____
• communication	• _____
• passionate	• _____
• executive presence	• _____
• persuasive	• _____

Weaknesses Assessment

MY WEAKNESSES	YOUR WEAKNESSES
• follow through	• _____
• perception of others	• _____
• attention to detail	• _____
• focus	• _____
• difficulty with decisions	• _____
• expectations of others	• _____
• hold grudges	• _____
• prioritization	• _____
• initial impressions	• _____
• narrowing my scope	• _____

I took this initial list and evaluated my different responses, understanding that not all of them are weighted equally. I am a much better communicator than a risk taker, but both represent areas in which I believed I excel. I started to prioritize. If it were something I was really good at, then I assigned it a high number (1-4). If I thought I was pretty good at something or could become better at something, then I listed it lower down the line (5-10).

I took this initial list and assigned my strengths a number ranging from one to the last number in sequence. I subsequently did the same for my weaknesses and then placed my results in sequential order.

Strengths Assessment (Sequential Order)

MY STRENGTHS	YOUR STRENGTHS
(1) idea generator	(1) _____
(2) relate well	(2) _____
(3) communication	(3) _____
(4) creativity	(4) _____
(5) risk taker	(5) _____
(6) executive presence	(6) _____
(7) persuasive	(7) _____
(8) passionate	(8) _____
(9) business acumen	(9) _____
(10) determined	(10) _____

Weaknesses Assessment (Sequential Order)

MY WEAKNESSES	YOUR WEAKNESSES
(1) follow through	(1) _____
(2) perception of others	(2) _____
(3) prioritization	(3) _____
(4) focus	(4) _____
(5) attention to detail	(5) _____
(6) difficulty with decisions	(6) _____
(7) expectations of others	(7) _____
(8) hold grudges	(8) _____
(9) initial impressions	(9) _____
(10) narrowing scope	(10) _____

If you are unable to come up with seven to ten responses, I recommend spending additional time completing this step. Remember, you are developing a networking plan for your career, so the amount of time invested in this will be reflected in your final work product.

The removal of external influences in the early stages of your self-assessment will likely result in questions like "Am I persuasive in a professional setting? Do I possess strong business acumen?" This is normal. The answer to these questions will be revealed when you are ready to solicit feedback and advice from outside parties after you have identified and prioritized your strengths and weaknesses.

(STOP!!!! DO NOT PROCEED UNTIL COMPLETED)

Step Two: Validate the results of your self-assessment with the assistance of trusted colleagues, personal friends and close family.

I began mentoring Andrew Kinn in 2012. Andrew was a graduate student at Ohio University who wanted to work in the front office for a professional sports franchise. During our initial conversations, he was convinced that he wanted to enter the business on the operations side in a personnel role. He was focused on learning more about the evaluation process and assessing professional talent as a scout. It is very difficult to gain experience in this area absent working for a professional organization or college athletics program. It is even more difficult if you also lack experience playing the sport in question. I advised Andrew of this.

I also took note of his abilities and strengths. He excelled in areas that I believed he could use to his advantage in searching for a position on the operations side of the business. One area in particular was statistics/analytics. While I was training him on all things related to the NFL salary cap, he would take phone calls from classmates desperate for guidance in his statistics course. It was pretty clear to me, based on his conversations with these other students that what Andrew did better than everyone else in his class was analytics.

I encouraged him to think of ways he could use analytics and statistics to improve player personnel, specifically the scouting process. Statistics was huge in the perceived individual sports, where different variables could be isolated and variances accounted for. But it wasn't as prevalent in professional football. Organizations such as the Jacksonville Jaguars and the San Francisco 49ers were moving in this direction and ahead of the curve, but many clubs were far behind. Andrew decided to pursue this route into an NFL front office.

Andrew began analyzing the roster moves of the 10 previous NFL Super Bowl champions as a way to develop content and establish his expertise in a particular area. He looked at the acquisition method (e.g. drafted, undrafted, free agency, etc.), starter composition and salary cap percentage allocations by position. His thesis was to identify a personnel structure and roster construction methodology that would offer a higher probability of success on the field. Andrew distributed his findings in the form of a white paper to various scouts and personnel executives.

Five months later, he was hired by the Green Bay Packers in an analytics role as a football operations/player personnel intern. It started as a one-year position, but by the end of the 2014 league year, he was a full-time employee.

*   *   *   *

Step Two of my self-assessment approach introduces the validation process. You need to identify two or three people in your life that know you well enough to provide you with what they believe are your strengths and weaknesses. Most people believe that they lack the necessary relationships to assist them in their careers. However, in most instances, this could not be further from the truth.

Look at your life from a global perspective. Identify the different circles of influence: social clubs, work committees, professional associations, etc. Within each circle of influence exists at least one person with whom you associate, someone that you have a heightened level of comfort around and trust to evaluate your talents and professional abilities. Request that these individuals provide you with an assessment of your strengths and weaknesses.

When requesting their feedback, be specific and make it known that their feedback will not hurt your feelings or impact your relationship. Their honesty and candidness in this process are crucial to the success of your self-assessment. Document their feedback in the same format utilized for your results. My initial lists from two of these individuals looked something like this:

Sibling's Assessment

STRENGTHS	WEAKNESSES
(1) drive	(1) lack of awareness
(2) sense of humor	(2) no work/life balance
(3) relate well with others	(3) time management
(4) spontaneity	(4) manage emotions
(5) creativity	(5) takes on too much
(6) intelligence	(6) follow through
(7) quick learner	

Co-worker's Assessment

STRENGTHS	WEAKNESSES
(1) dreamer	(1) too casual at times
(2) motivator	(2) uses humor as go to
(3) self-initiating	(3) lack of self-promotion
(4) strong work ethic	(4) follow through
(5) great people skills	(5) inconsistent effort
(6) energetic/enthusiastic	(6) procrastination
(7) quick learner	(7) impatient with follow-up
(8) thinks outside the box	(8) change in leadership
(9) business acumen	
(10) determined	

Similar to your own results, these individuals should provide you with as many relevant, accurate responses as possible in each category. Ideally, this will be between seven and ten traits or skill sets. If they did not provide at least five strengths and weaknesses, I recommend requesting additional feedback. The alternative is to rely on commercial resources to obtain this information. These commercial options include StrengthFinders 2.0, Myers Briggs Test, or Personalysis. These can be helpful, but there is no substitute for candid feedback from the people that know you best. Make it a priority to get this information first-hand.

As soon as you receive their feedback, process this information. Don't be afraid to follow up and ask specific questions. There is more value in understanding their responses than simply receiving them. Once you've had a chance to discuss the results with them, ask these individuals to list your strengths and weaknesses in sequential order. Doing so will help you compare their responses with your results.

Step Three: Compare and contrast to identify your top responses in each category.

Step Three is about narrowing your focus and identifying the common responses in each category. There is a saying I often think about that goes, "If you spend your life trying to be good at everything, you will never be great at anything." At the heart of this quote is the principle that drives this step of the self-assessment process, which is a narrow focus and identification of what you do best.

Another reason this is so important is alluded to in most of the contributor chapters in this book. The sports industry has become more sophisticated over the years, and it is no longer possible to enter the business as a perceived "generalist." Alec Scheiner expressly acknowledges this. Kevin Abrams and Ethan Waugh encourage readers to focus on what they are good at and ultimately responsible for, which is presumably why the organization hired the person.

Perform a side-by-side analysis of your results and the strengths and weaknesses identified by the individuals selected to provide you with candid feedback. Pay close attention to the strengths and weaknesses you listed as numbers 1-5. Ideally, the results align. This comparison revealed my top five strengths and weaknesses.

Top Strengths and Weaknesses

MY STRENGTHS	MY WEAKNESSES
(1) idea generator - visionary	(1) follow through
(2) relate well - relate to others	(2) self-promotion
(3) articulation/communication	(3) prioritization
(4) business acumen	(4) focus
(5) passion/determination	(5) scheduling/multi-tasking

YOUR STRENGTHS	YOUR WEAKNESSES
(1) _____	(1) _____
(2) _____	(2) _____
(3) _____	(3) _____
(4) _____	(4) _____
(5) _____	(5) _____

If the results do not align, take a minute and assess the differences. Have a conversation with these individuals. There are no right or wrong answers. *The definition of success for this process is a clear understanding of what you do best and the areas you will need to work on improving and gain support to succeed.* The last step in this process is identifying what role(s) are best suited by your strengths.

Step Four: Identify the position(s) in the industry that best fit your interests and your strongest skill sets.

Once you identify your primary strengths and weaknesses, you can begin to identify the position(s) that best fit your skill sets and interests. Failing to align the two prior to the construction of your networking plan and search for a career reduces the likelihood of success in a particular role. You want to position yourself for success starting with your first position in the industry.

As a graduate student, I approached various professionals for the sole purpose of learning about their careers and responsibilities as a salary cap analyst/general manager/attorney for an organization in the Big Four. I found that my success rate for connecting with these individuals was much higher when I positioned my introduction as a way to learn more about them and their careers, as opposed to an introduction about myself. This is implied in the former approach.

I learned a lot and was able to identify the position(s) that I should pursue if I wanted experience with the salary cap and player contract negotiations. By way of an example, I assumed that the club's attorney handled the majority of player contract negotiations and salary cap related-issues, since these areas are governed by the NFL's Collective Bargaining Agreement. I came to learn through these conversations that a club's counsel very rarely involves himself or herself in player contract negotiations. Instead, most attorneys for professional sports teams focus on handling labor and employment matters, managing litigation against the club with outside counsel, implementing revenue-producing activities (e.g. executing agreements, addressing liability concerns, etc.) and serving as the club's liaison on league-wide issues.

Equipped with this information, I narrowed my focus and networking approach to the individuals responsible for the salary cap and player contracts for each club and moved away from focusing solely on connecting with attorneys. It was still beneficial to meet with professionals occupying different roles, but if I were going to connect and establish a relationship with decision-makers over the salary cap and player contracts, I had to focus on connecting with these professionals with each club.

Speaking with these individuals taught me that successful salary cap analysts and agents alike are very detail oriented and thrive when they can juggle multiple tasks. I already knew that these were two attributes identified as my weaknesses, so I would need to work on improving in those areas in order to position myself for success in both roles. I prioritized improvement in these two areas while I continued to network.

The last task in this chapter is for you to identify your position(s) of interest and then determine if they align with your skill sets. Perform your own research. Identify people occupying the position(s) of your interest and gather as much information as you can from them regarding their daily responsibilities and what it takes to succeed in that particular role.

As you learn what it takes to succeed in a specific position, compare these findings to your strengths and weaknesses assessments. Identify your position(s) of interest and write them in the space provided. If they do not align with your strengths, start thinking of ways that you can improve in specific areas that are considered your weaknesses.

15

DEVELOP: CONSTRUCTING YOUR OWN NETWORKING PLAN

I created my own networking approach to obtain my first position in the sports industry. I determined what helped me connect with others and eliminated attempts and approaches that weren't as successful. Most importantly, advice from members of my network influenced my approach. What resulted is this networking plan focused on building the right relationships in the industry that helped launch my career, which will in turn help you do the same.

The DEVELOP component of my networking plan consists of three steps.

1. Contacts
2. Content
3. Value Added

Each component requires time, dedication and creative planning. Regardless of your experience level, the first step can begin immediately following the completion of your self-assessment with the creation of your personal contact list.

Step One: Develop your contact list.

My initial contact list included every salary cap analyst, VP of football/baseball/basketball/hockey administration and general manager in the Big Four. Significant emphasis was placed on connecting with the individuals occupying these roles in the National Football League.

The construction of your contact list starts with the identification of the different pieces of information you want to include that will help facilitate a conversation. Information such as name, organization, title, phone number and email are a must. But listing these individuals and the mandatory information fields is just the start of a more complex, detail-specific contact list. *The overall objective is to create an elaborate, carefully developed contact list that contains enough information to draft an email or facilitate a conversation that welcomes a response*.

Personalizing your list will take some additional time and require more work, but this level of information is absolutely necessary to connect at a much deeper level. I did whatever I could to link people together and find a reason for that person to respond. Include information such as community involvement, personal passions, previous employers and career accomplishments. Another field that will add value is an "Ally" category, which will list a person that can help you build a relationship with that sports professional. A successful contact list should help you connect the dots and link people throughout the industry.

It is important to finalize your template by identifying the different types of information you will need before reaching out to the individuals on your list. Once you are comfortable with the different fields and your contact list template is finalized, the next step is locating the different pieces of information. Contact information can be very difficult to come by in professional sports. Most colleges post staff directories and other sources of contact information, but professional sports teams do not. This increases the difficulty in obtaining this information at the professional level.

I visited every team's website and staff web pages in search of this information. At the very least, you will be able to fill in the name, position, organization, and limited personal information from a published biography. From there, obtaining contact information is a bit of a scavenger hunt. Social media sites such as Linked or Twitter might help you get this information, but most of it will come from the individual or someone close to the person. I mastered the art of repurposing email addresses early on in my information gathering process.

I would flip through organization directories and other club contact sheets in search of any employee with an organization in the NFL. If John Doe, who happened to work in sales for the Cleveland Browns, had an email address of doej@cleveland.dogpound.com, then chances are the organization's email structure is "last name followed by first letter of first name" @cleveland.dogpound.com. I would substitute the person's name I wanted to contact in that format. Most of the time, this approach was successful. If I didn't get a bounce-back email, then I was fairly confident my message reached their inbox.

Phone numbers are a little more difficult to obtain. The best way to get this information is to call the main line and request to be connected with a specific employee. The switchboard will almost always connect you via instant transfer, but few will provide you with the direct number. At the outset, focus on gathering the primary phone number for the organizations. When the time comes to make these phone calls, request the person's direct number. If the front desk will not provide this information, keep a pen handy. Personal extensions and other information are often included in the voicemail prompt or the transfer communication.

The information that will help you personalize your list may be even more difficult to come by. If you find that your sheet lacks substance other than name, organization, position and contact information, you will need to be creative and find ways to obtain additional data. Here are a few suggestions and techniques that helped me and may help you.

> • **Join sports clubs, discussion boards and professional interest groups** – There are various groups and associations with a focus on different segments in the sports industry. Before joining these clubs or associations, conduct research and ask specific questions. How many members? How much is a membership? Do the events cost additional money? And, most importantly, does it have a membership

directory? I joined the Sports Lawyers Association solely for the membership directory.

Various social media sites offer professional interest groups and discussion boards with open memberships and active participation. Become acclimated with each group's purpose and the content that is frequently posted. Participation in these conversations will lead to side discussions and help establish yourself as an expert in the area of your interest. Different organizations available to sports professionals include the Sport Marketing Association, National Sales Network, and Sports Lawyers Association, among others.

• **Create an organization** – I formed the Sports Law Committee for the Columbus Bar Association. The attendance at my monthly meetings rarely exceeded 10 participants. However, I was responsible for engaging speakers every month, which gave me a reason to reach out to different people in sports with whom I had yet to form a relationship. This helped me maintain, and grow, my network. Some of my speakers included Steve Fehr, Special Counsel for the NHLPA; Alec Scheiner, who at the time was SVP and General Counsel for the Dallas Cowboys; and Leah Rinfret, Executive Counsel for the Women's Tennis Association.

When starting an organization or a group, I recommend approaching established professional organizations that would benefit from another committee or subject matter expert. These organizations likely have the available resources and can assist with coordinating meetings, building relationships and reaching out to professionals in the community. It also provides you with a greater sense of legitimacy in the eyes of the participants.

• **Attend industry-related events** – Research the different events that attract a large number of industry professionals and make it a priority to attend the events within driving distance. The event itself isn't as important as the attendees at the event. Make an effort to schedule as many meet and greets as possible at these functions, understanding that a large majority of them will get cancelled or postponed. I attend the NFL Combine on an annual basis. I also traveled to events outside my direct interest, including the Winter Baseball Meeting, NHL All-Star Break and the NCAA Final Four. The important thing to remember is to attend these events as an aspiring professional, not as a fan. Admittedly, I forgot this at times (typically at the Final Four).

• **Volunteer** – Get involved. Look for local opportunities that will help you connect with sports professionals in the area. I volunteered for the Capital Hockey Conference, a youth hockey league that was led by the Columbus Blue Jackets' Senior Vice President & General Counsel, Greg Kirstein. I knew that Greg was passionate about this organization and was strapped for time. I also knew Greg was very well connected in the local community and in the sports industry. When he informed me that he wouldn't have a legal internship available with the Blue Jackets, I immediately volunteered for the Capital Hockey Conference. I got to know Greg on a more personal level, and, to this day, Greg remains a valuable member of my network.

I started with *one* person on my contact list. These approaches and the tips that follow have helped me develop a very expansive list that well exceeds 500+ professionals in different capacities across the sports industry. It is important to remember that this is an ongoing process. It does not have an end date, and if you use it properly, it will not get outdated. While you develop your list early in the process, you should be using these individuals to assist with developing your content.

TIPS FOR CONSTRUCTING A WELL-DEVELOPED CONTACT LIST

1. Identify your desired positions(s). If there are differences across the sports leagues, adjust your list to account for these differences and pursue the organizations that offer this type of position.

2. Finalize the data fields on your list that will help you personalize your approach.

3. Establish a priority system for the contacts maintained on your list.

4. Update the field with the date that you last communicated.

5. Designate a "notes" section to record content of recent conversations.

Step Two: Establish and build your content.

The term "content" encompasses the projects, initiatives and accomplishments that display your substantive knowledge and expertise in a particular area of the industry. Your content is what will drive conversations, create relationships and establish credibility in the industry.

The importance of developing content really stood out when I reviewed emails I had sent over the years to various executives. I didn't have content when I started networking. I approached my career like most young professionals: where I wanted to be and not how I would get there. I was under the mistaken belief that people would just respond to my emails because I had a solid educational background and the rest would take care of itself. Again, I was naïve. The following excerpt is from an email I sent early in the process of securing my first job in the sports industry.

"Dear Rocco:

My name is Justin Hunt, and I am currently completing my Masters of Sports Administration at Ohio University. Ed Malone (PD) recommended that I send you my résumé concerning <u>the positions available</u> with the Tampa Bay Buccaneers. I am very interested in the football operations side of the business, specifically dealing with the salary cap and/or legal counsel issues. I am a licensed attorney in the State of Ohio with a <u>limited background</u> in contract law. I hope this email finds you well, and I thank you in advance for <u>any assistance</u> you are able to provide through your connections with the Buccaneers.

Best Regards,

Justin R. Hunt"

As the language in my email suggests, I lacked content and vision. The underlined language provides specific examples where I am non-committal and very general with my approach. This is a great example of what not to do when drafting a networking email. I sent similar emails to local sports agencies and attorneys that worked in sports looking for volunteer opportunities. What I thought at the time conveyed passion and potential, in fact, displayed desperation.

It wasn't until I published different law review articles and established myself as someone knowledgeable in the salary cap and revenue sharing models in professional sports that I started to make progress and receive responses from executives and sports agents. I had a selling point. I had content. These articles supported my strengths and knowledge of the business. The following excerpt is an email I sent to a general manager in the NFL after the publication of my legal note.

"Mr. XXX:

First, I would like to congratulate you on your recent promotion to General Manager. This is an amazing accomplishment, and I wish you the best of luck in this role.

After reading an article covering your path into the National Football League, I can't help but notice the similarities in our beginnings. I have been rejected by almost every team in the National Football League, some two or three times. I interviewed with teams, attended the NFL Combine, met numerous salary cap administrators, and spoke with Assistant General Managers. Many think that I am just another young kid chasing a dream, but I offer something very different, and my experience can attest to that. The following distinguishes me from other applicants:

- Licensed attorney in the State of Ohio eligible to serve as legal counsel for organizations in all 50 states.
- Contracted to publish my legal note covering the case of *American Needle v. National Football League* in the University of Virginia's Sports and Entertainment Law Journal.

- Enhanced my understanding of the 30% rule, LTBE and NLTBE incentives, and the strategic use of signing bonuses as it relates to player compensation while completing my legal note.

- Obtained my Masters of Sports Administration from Ohio University, regarded as the country's leading graduate program in this field.

- Currently helping a company develop a player evaluation tool comparing salary and statistical performance levels.

I hope the above examples provide you with a better understanding of my experiences, abilities and interests as they relate to player finances and legal issues. I have attached my résumé for you to review at your leisure. I look forward to your response and setting up a call in the near future.

Regards,

Justin R. Hunt"

The time lapse between the first email and the second email was six months. I was working towards an additional degree and published a legal note on the NFL's salary cap. Otherwise, my situation was the same in both instances. The difference was I positioned myself as someone with knowledge in a specific area of the NFL that would benefit the organization, and specifically, the part of the organization for which the recipient was responsible.

When reaching out to the individuals on your list, you need something to keep them interested and make them want to help. The different volunteer projects and self-driven initiatives that you work on will serve as the foundation for your content early in your career. Keep a running list of projects and tasks that will equip you with additional content.

There are always opportunities to develop your content. Here are a few suggestions:

- **Research emerging industry trends** – Regardless of your specific career interest, industries are constantly changing. The best way to develop content is to identify emerging trends, technologies or business transactions and become an expert in these areas. The focus of my legal note was two areas with significant uncertainty: the NFL's Collective Bargaining Agreement and the impact the Court's ruling in *American Needle* would have on player salaries. Industry professionals were interested in both of these areas, so I was credited for finding a way to merge the two and determine how one would impact the other.

Another good example is Andrew Kinn's paper on the roster composition of the previous 10 Super Bowl Champions. His paper introduced analytics to roster make-up, which was something new to some of the executives who received his paper.

My contributors threw out a few ideas with respect to how they see their roles changing in sports. This is a starting point. Research these trends and start to think how this will impact the professional sports league of your interest. If you don't have an answer to this question yet, continue to network with individuals that understand a particular aspect of the business. Use these relationships to develop your understanding.

• **Rely on your network to develop your content** – You have to take a different angle than the "I need a job" approach that is all too common with industry professionals. I found that networking is much easier when you request assistance with understanding their area of the business. The executives that helped me draft my different legal notes remain close to me, and a few of them participated in this collaboration. This is another example of being creative and relying on these individuals to develop content. If you do this right, they also become influential members of your network.

• **Volunteer to assist industry professionals with interest projects** – One thing holds particularly true for employees in the sports industry. They work very long hours and have very little time for extracurricular activities and personal interest projects. So help them. Many professionals write articles and pursue outside employment activities that require assistance. One specific example is Brian Gainor's website, www.partnershipactivations.com. Brian requested the assistance of students and professionals alike to share sponsorship activation ideas, trends and best practices. A few of my friends assisted Brian early in his development of this website and quarterly newsletter.

Identifying these opportunities can be difficult early on, but you can take certain steps to position yourself to learn about them. One way to hear about these opportunities is to make it known to the members of your network that you are looking for ways to gain experience and develop your understanding in a particular area. Kindly request that they think of you and inform you if/when they learn of these opportunities. This is how I learned about a salary cap project across the Big Four that required me to learn each league's salary cap rules. Also, pay attention to discussion boards and social media sites. This is another way that individuals and companies advertise similar opportunities and projects.

The first two steps are inextricably linked, meaning that in order to develop content, you will need contacts that will assist you with gaining this exposure in the industry. In order to build a strong, diverse contact list, you will need content stemming from your experiences. A perfect example of this relationship and how these priorities are interrelated is this book and the process of securing my different contributors.

As you develop your content, focus on ways to add members to your contact list, and as you add more contacts, look to keep them involved, and interested, by assisting with the development of your content. This is the best way to keep your contacts engaged and vested in your professional pursuits. The experiences through which you establish your content will also help you identify your value added.

Step Three: Communicate your value added.

The final component of DEVELOP focuses more on how you present yourself to others and how you are perceived as a potential candidate for a job. Identifying your value added will help put you in a position to approach decision makers with a confident understanding of your strengths and abilities.

Jason Selk referred to your value added as "that one thing that you do better than anyone else that will increase the organization's bottom line." According to Alec Scheiner, "The business has evolved and so have the professionals working in the industry, so you need a particular skill set just to get into the business." Ideally your value added is the skill set that will land your first role in sports.

My value added became relatively clear to me after taking a step back. My approach was too broad in the beginning, so I needed to narrow my focus. I thought to myself before becoming a sports agent, "What differentiates me from other aspiring agents looking for similar opportunities?" I had my law degree, but the majority of aspiring and active agents did as well. My network of scouts and personnel in the NFL was very strong, but many of the experienced agents also had great connections in the industry. I had experience working in an NFL front office – very few active agents and aspiring agents could say the same. That experience was something I could bring to the table that most firms lacked.

Understanding the economics of the NFL, the salary cap and player contracts are essential to becoming a successful sports agent. However, in one's role as an agent, this experience is limited in the early stages and only gained through representing NFL players. I removed this barrier by working in the 49ers' front office, so this was my competitive advantage over other aspiring NFL agents. This became my central focus when engaging potential employers.

My value added: My understanding of the NFL salary cap, collective bargaining agreement and the NFL's player compensation model will improve an organization's approach to recruiting prospects, setting the market for contract negotiations and negotiating player contracts.

It is very difficult to identify your value added early in your career. This challenge was reflected in the networking emails sent early in my search for a position in professional sports. As you develop content and an understanding of the different positions, you will start to see where you can add value and where you would be a waste of resources.

Identifying these areas is the first step. You also need to understand how what you do best will improve an organization or solve a problem that currently exists. This can be difficult without exposure to the organization and this type of work. Conversations with members of your network will help you understand where improvements can be made, but the onus is on you to identify and subsequently pursue these areas.

Your value added will need to be very specific and should be the result of the content you've developed along the way. Say goodbye to the catch-all objective statement on your résumé. A strong value added statement draws a connection between your strengths and the responsibilities of the position. Draft your initial value-added statement in the space provided. This statement will change frequently, so it is important that you continually revisit this statement and revise when necessary as you develop your content and position yourself for a career in the sports industry.

ELEMENTS OF A STRONG VALUE-ADDED STATEMENT

1. Draft a concise, narrowly-focused conveyance of what you do best.

2. Incorporate the requirement(s) of the desired role that your strength(s) satisfy, i.e., how this will benefit the organization.

3. Use action verbs and language focused on continued improvement to accomplish a specific goal.

16

IMPLEMENT: STAY YOUR COURSE AND DON'T LOOK BACK

The implementation of your networking plan requires commitment and determination. If you followed my approach laid out in the preceding chapters, you have enough information to start making phone calls and sending emails to connect with the individuals on your contact list. It is important to understand that your initial attempts to contact these individuals will likely result in minimal success.

As you meet different people and develop your content, you will eventually start to make progress on your list. The success rate of your cold calls and email inquiries will slowly rise and your network will thrive. I spent the better part of three years connecting with people and positioning myself for an opportunity with an NFL team. My approach varied depending on the individual and job title, but it was always made clear that what I sought was information and advice, not a job.

The advice you receive from these individuals will shed light on the required skill sets to succeed in a particular role. You will learn what tasks will equip you with the necessary skills and, more importantly, what you can do to prepare for a specific role in sports. When I started making phone calls, I kept a journal and recorded my conversations. My notes included personal information, professional advice and career recommendations. This information was very valuable and helped me develop a plan that would accomplish my career objectives.

Before you make any phone calls, use a separate notebook for the sole purpose of recording conversations with the individuals on your contact list. This will help keep all of this information in one location. As you make progress, consider the following advice to help you stay on track and develop a strong, diverse network of professionals that will benefit your career for years to come.

1. Build Your "A Network" Through Multiple Interactions: Follow Up Is Key

First impressions are very important. But with respect to networking and building a strong network, it is often the steps you take after the initial introduction that strengthens relationships. A lack of follow-up makes one easy to forget, instead of easy to help. To illustrate this, think of the last time you met someone and spoke with him or her for 15-30 minutes. What was that person's name? What did he or she do for a living? Having a hard time remembering? Medical professionals suggest that the brain naturally disposes of information. Follow-up is the best way to commit your name to memory and a solution to this natural occurrence.

Successful follow up gets easier as you accomplish more in the industry, and your list of contacts expands. The fact of the matter is you need something to talk about the second time around. Otherwise, you leave the person wondering, "Why in the heck is this person reaching out to me again?" This question is a networker's worst nightmare.

I rely on my content (e.g. graduate degree, publications, front office experience, volunteer projects, this book, etc.) to have greater success with my follow up. I would focus on certain individuals in my network with strong ties to the salary cap and player contracts as I looked to schedule subsequent conversations. This is something I always did, but it wasn't until Andy Dolich referred to this as "developing your 'A Network'" that I included this as part of my networking plan for readers.

Identify 10 people on your contact list that you hope to include in your "A Network", recognizing that your end goal is to secure five of them. If this doesn't work out, identify others with similar qualities and experiences that can take the place of the original 10 that you identified. Once you connect with five, focus your efforts on building a strong relationship with them while still connecting with others to broaden the scope of your network. Consistency in your follow up needs to be a high priority. The following tips should help you secure the initial five professionals in your "A Network."

• **Develop a reliable tracking system** – Design a tracking sheet to help manage your contacts. Be sure to track the last date of contact or last conversation, as well as the contents of that conversation. For me, I developed a Microsoft Excel sheet that would turn a person's name green if I hadn't spoken with him or her in 6 months and red if it had been 12 months.

• **Prepare for your initial conversation** – The majority of questions asked during the initial conversation should be professional in nature. Remember, the goal is to learn more about the person's role in the organization and the specific responsibilities that the position of your interest entails. You should learn something new about the position of your interest with every phone call. As the call is winding down, don't be afraid to ask about family, personal interests, etc. If your research revealed some commonality, bring it up and ask additional questions in this area. This personal information will help with follow-up conversations.

• **Plan a networking trip** – A face-to-face meeting goes a long way. Find a city or multiple cities close in proximity that have different individuals that you would like to engage with and send a few email feelers assessing their availability to meet in person. I coordinated over five networking trips when I first started my search. Sometimes they involved a sporting event, but other times the sole purpose for my trip was to meet with these individuals.

• **Track important dates** – Reach out when an important date is approaching. The event isn't as important as the gesture, but it helps if the event is something the person is very passionate about. These events might include the birth of a child, work anniversary, career promotion or a specific personal accomplishment. Use this note to acknowledge that you look forward to connecting with him/her again and getting further acquainted.

• **Provide a meaningful update** – As you begin connecting with professionals at the higher levels, meaningless emails or phone calls will drive them away and make it less likely that they will help you. Derrick Hall cautioned against providing too many updates. This is another reason why it is so important to track your conversations and the dates of those conversations. It is possible to over-network, so be certain to make these updates meaningful and relevant.

I recommend creating a follow-up column in your contact list. Record simple, one-word follow-up ideas. A few examples include triathlete, charity or faith to help trigger a potential successful follow-up approach. Keep detailed notes in your comments section regarding your approach.

As I developed strong relationships with a select few, our conversations became more candid and resembled conversations that a mentor would have with his/her mentee, as opposed to a cold call or introduction. That is the goal! These mentors started throwing out ideas that might help me get where I wanted to be. For example, they advised me to get experience working in an NFL front office before becoming a sports agent and to publish articles on the salary cap to display my knowledge of the NFL's business model before seeking a job in an NFL front office.

These recommendations served as early benchmarks for me to accomplish. These tasks became the first step in a tiered approach that would help me realize my career objectives and develop a strategic approach to get there. This approach became my Next Level List.

2.   The Next Level List

The Next Level List identifies certain benchmarks that, if achieved, will collectively lead to the accomplishment of a specific career objective. The majority of professionals are too overwhelmed with current responsibilities to remain focused on the next step in their professional careers. This is even truer for professionals considering a career transition. And not everyone can afford an executive coach. However, losing sight of your long-term goals can sidetrack your progress towards obtaining these objectives or, even worse, prevent you from ever reaching them.

I started experimenting with these lists during my graduate studies at Ohio University. I had some lofty goals, but I realized that I did nothing to make them come to fruition beyond getting a good education. So I started to write down everything that I wanted to accomplish. My initial list looked something like this.

- Publish a book covering my career and path to becoming an agent.

- Lead an athlete representation firm.

- Form a charity impacting a cause near and dear to my heart.

- Become one of the most well-connected professionals in the sports industry.

- Give back and make a difference in the lives of others.

Such an ambitious list can be outright intimidating and have the exact opposite effect from its intended purpose. I recall sitting in the coffee shop on the second floor of Alden Library in Athens, Ohio, and thinking to myself, "What is the best way to accomplish all my goals?" My initial list was also very broad and too difficult to measure my success in pursuit of these goals. What I did next became the solution to my initial concerns and the foundation of this Next Level List concept.

I created a sub-list for every objective by working backwards. I identified which tasks would help me achieve the desired outcome and prioritized them into action items. Advice from members of my network, a plethora of independent research and, at times, plain common sense helped me determine the best approach. These action items were separated into two categories: *short-term goals* and *long-term goals*. As a rule of thumb, short-term goals should be achievable within one-to-three years. Long-term goals should be obtainable within three-to-five years, allowing flexibility for achievement.

When I created my first official Next Level List drafted with an eye towards becoming a sports agent, my list looked like this.

Goals & Career Objectives

SHORT-TERM GOALS

(1) Establish at least one contact in each of the 32 NFL organizations.
(2) Publish a legal note covering the NFL's salary cap and revenue sharing.
(3) Pass the NFLPA's Agent Certification Exam.

LONG-TERM GOALS

(1) Obtain an entry-level salary cap position with an NFL organization.
(2) Represent NFL players in contract negotiations & marketing and endorsement deals.

CAREER OBJECTIVES

(1) Become CEO and President of an elite athlete and executive representation firm.

While these lists provide actionable items with real deadlines, they should be structured in such a way that allows for some flexibility. Designating an action item as "short term" or "long term" won't always dictate the order in which your accomplishments occur. I believed it would take me longer to get a position in an NFL front office than it would for me to become certified as an NFL agent, but that wasn't the case. Revisiting this list and making changes when necessary is just as important as putting your goals on paper.

To that same end, the goals and objectives you envision early in your career will change as you learn the business and identify what positions align with your strengths. This is also true when you learn that a position you imagined isn't quite what you thought it would be. If your career objective changes based on your experiences, toss the list and begin another. *Every experience can be leveraged and used as progress towards a new career objective.*

The Next Level List is a mechanism designed to help you focus on your career objectives and the steps you need to take to reach them. This concept applies to both personal and professional goals. So get creative. In the illustration provided below, identify your most important career objective and create your first Next Level List.

Goals & Career Objectives

SHORT-TERM GOALS

LONG-TERM GOALS

CAREER OBJECTIVES

3.   The 30-Day Challenge

The 30-day challenge was introduced to me in law school. The concept, as it was explained, is simple. Identify something you want to do every day for 30 days. The scope can range from fitness goals to professional accomplishments. This approach to goal setting and high performance didn't really resonate with me at first.

As I developed my own networking plan and approach to personal and professional development, I tweaked this idea of a 30-day challenge and used it as a tool to measure my performance and prevent me from navigating away from my Next Level List. Instead of identifying something that I wanted to do for 30 days, my focus shifted to things that could be accomplished in 30 days. I set short-term, 30-day objectives that collectively would achieve the short-term goals on my Next Level List. This created a level of accountability on a daily basis.

Over time, the 30-day challenge became a staple of my development plan and part of my daily routine. I began setting consecutive 30-day challenges in different aspects of my career and personal life. For instance, one of my first career objectives was to establish at least one point of contact in each of the 32 NFL organizations. With this objective in mind, I set out with the following 30-day challenge:

- Email at least one person per day that works directly with the NFL's salary cap and revenue sharing model.

- Allocate 30 minutes towards researching the backgrounds of salary cap managers in the NFL.

- Spend 30 minutes researching the collective bargaining process and player contract negotiations.

Collectively, these three tasks could be performed in approximately one hour. This seemed pretty simple, and that is the idea. I did these three things for 30 days, and at the end of the 30-day challenge, I had a better understanding of the collective bargaining process and a strong foundation in the NFL's salary cap and player contract negotiations. My calendar had a few calls scheduled with professionals that work with the salary cap, which would help me better understand these areas of the NFL's business model.

Subsequent 30-day challenges leveraged my progress from a previous challenge and put me in a position to start writing this article. Six months later, my article, "Why single is better: The implications of a multi-entity ruling on revenue sharing and the NFL salary cap," was published. For me, this approach really worked.

These same relationships that helped me publish two legal notes on this subject matter also helped me connect with others in the industry responsible for the salary cap, which was another short-term objective in my Next Level List to become CEO of a representation firm. I shifted the focus of subsequent 30-day challenges and prioritized (a) becoming certified as an NFL agent or (b) securing a position in an NFL front office. When I received my offer from the 49ers, my initial Next Level List resembled the following illustration:

Goals & Career Objectives

SHORT-TERM GOALS

(1) Establish at least one contact in each of the 32 NFL organizations.
(2) Publish a legal note covering the NFL's salary cap and revenue sharing.
(3) Pass the NFLPA's Agent Certification Exam.

LONG-TERM GOALS

(1) Obtain an entry-level salary cap position with an NFL organization.
(2) Represent NFL players in contract negotiations & marketing and endorsement deals.

CAREER OBJECTIVES

(1) Become CEO and President of an elite athlete and executive representation firm.

In San Francisco, I had to balance doing my job while making progress towards becoming an NFL agent. My 30-day challenges included forming relationships with active NFL agents and learning the intricacies of player contracts while I occupied a front office position. This approach helped me partner with Sterling Sports Management and serve as Director of Football Operations following my tenure with the San Francisco 49ers.

Fast forward to today. My very first Next Level List is nearing completion, as I subsequently became certified by the NFLPA and represented various professional football players in contracts and marketing negotiations. All that is left on this particular Next Level List is for me to become CEO/President of an athlete representation firm, which I will do.

My success in the industry is partially the result of my commitment to the Next Level List and 30-day challenges. For these to be effective, they must be prepared and executed properly.

First, the tasks identified should be realistic and, ideally, quantifiable. If not, you will not complete the challenge and your progress will be deterred. Second, tracking your progress at different intervals is very important. I do this weekly. You can choose to do this more frequently if you like. Reviewing your performance will help you determine if you are on track to meet a specific target, or if you need to adjust your daily output to accomplish your 30-day challenge.

I also document my results on a 2x3 poster board. This helps me identify my most productive time periods and days during the week. Finally, you need to identify the tasks and assignments, the completion of which would satisfy multiple objectives or result in your acquiring skill sets applicable in various positions. The phrase "kill two birds with one stone" is cliché, but that's exactly what you need to do. This is especially true for those looking to transition roles or start from scratch in pursuit of a position in another industry.

Later in my professional career, I introduced this concept to a team of attorneys at a Fortune 100 Company. A request was made that each member of the team submit one thing that they wanted to do for 30 days. The submissions varied from spend one hour painting every day to run three miles every day for 30 days. At the end of the 30-day period, the team reconvened. It was difficult to get initial buy-in from everyone involved, but for those that participated, there was an immediate increase in engagement and personal accountability. The general outlook was positive. By testing this approach with multiple people in various professions, I was able to validate that 30-day challenges work, regardless of the industry.

This also proves that 30-day challenges and my Next Level List can be used at any point in your career. Experienced professionals, young professionals, students and/or retirees can use these tools. They are effective with career advancement or career transitions. In the space provided below, create one example of a 30-day challenge that you will complete using the following tips.

COMPONENTS OF A SUCCESSFUL 30-DAY CHALLENGE

1. Write down a list of things that you hope to accomplish in a 30-day span. Consider the short-term goals in your Next Level List(s) and identify what you need to accomplish now to get to that point.

2. Narrow this list to two or three things that you determine are realistic, obtainable outcomes in a 30-day period.

3. Ensure that the results of each 30-day challenge are quantifiable and measurable, e.g. do something daily for a set time, run a set distance, etc.

4. Develop a tracking system that monitors your performance and determines if you will meet your 30-day challenge.

5. Continue the momentum gained from a 30-day challenge to implement another challenge that collectively will lead to your short-term objective(s).

CONCLUSION

You have the ability to develop a networking plan that will help you acquire the necessary skills and develop a strong foundational network that will assist you when pursuing your dream job and accomplishing your professional goals. The specific focus of my book is the sports industry, but the principles that comprise my networking plan have general application. The ASSESS, DEVELOP, IMPLEMENT approach, if applied consistently, will lead to the relationships and the knowledge of the industry that you need to land a particular role.

I've come a long way since my initial phone call with Kevin Abrams, but I've only scratched the surface. The relationships that I've formed over the past five years are real, and my early successes likely wouldn't have happened without these strong relationships. My network will continue to be an integral part of my career, regardless of my next professional move.

But I didn't just start with these relationships. I began this collaboration with one contributor. Over time, I was able to convince 11 high-level executives to commit their time and tell their stories to aspiring professionals by utilizing the strategies described in this book.

As you embark on your journey, it is natural to be intimidated by industry executives in the early stages of building your network. When I tell my story, people ask, "How did you work up the courage to approach these professionals?" My answer is preparation. The level of preparation that goes into creating your contact list, building content and developing your networking plan provides a foundation that carries a level of comfort and familiarity when approaching these individuals. It also helps facilitate introductions and subsequent conversations. That is why it is so important to commit to my networking plan.

Pay particularly close attention to my contributors' advice. What they offer is position-specific feedback based on their experiences in the position(s) you desire to hold. Their paths into the industry represent one way to obtain a specific position, but it is not the only way. Instead of focusing solely on their path into the industry, consider their recommendations and suggestions on what the future holds for their area of sports. This type of forward thinking represents your best odds of securing a particular position.

From start to finish, it took me the better part of four years to finish this book. It took me much longer to develop the content necessary to author this work. And now I am down to my last few paragraphs. For years, I've thought about how I would conclude. In the end, it became very apparent. I conclude with a simple reminder that life is a journey. Be certain to enjoy YOUR journey.

It is easy to become distracted with career goals and forget that there is more to life than professional accomplishments. I practice law, represent professional athletes and coaches, consult on sports business and advise professionals in different industries, among other things. I have a family with one beautiful child and another on the way. I enjoy travel and other personal pursuits. My point is that life is busy, but if you live it right, you learn to enjoy every minute of it. My mother constantly reminds me, "Stay in the moment. Be where you are when you are there." I struggle with this daily, but it is something I focus on improving and encourage you to do the same. Enjoy the journey.

As you move forward, set some lofty expectations for yourself. I've set very high goals for myself. I do this because I refuse to let fear dictate my career pursuits. Don't let a fear of rejection prevent you from pursuing your dream job. In the end, failing to achieve a dream you attempt is so much more rewarding than never pursuing it. Continuously remind yourself to never give up. And when the path is so daunting you're not sure what to do next, just remember...it all starts with a phone call.

ACKNOWLEDGEMENTS

This book wouldn't have been possible without the love, support and encouragement of many.

To my wife, Bryn. Your love, support, partnership and selflessness greatly exceed what any words or sentiments can convey in these pages. This book and my professional accomplishments highlighted throughout are just as much yours as they are mine. You are a fantastic wife, mother, sister, daughter and friend. I couldn't have picked a better "teammate" to join me on this crazy journey called life.

To my children. I've held numerous titles in my short lifetime, including Chief Legal Counsel, Senior Counsel, NFL Agent, Salary Cap Administrator and now Author. The most rewarding, but challenging, title of all is DAD. You encourage me to work harder, be better and enjoy the simple things in life. Stay young at heart and remember that life is a journey, and you control YOUR journey. Just as my mother told me, "You Choose Which Party to Attend." Always remember this.

To my mother, Carol. A talented language arts teacher by trade; a loving mother at heart. You spent an entire career advocating and verbally teaching students at every level, but your greatest teaching moments are non-verbal. You raised three children, influenced hundreds of students and encouraged thousands of people to see the good in everything and make the best of every situation. My wish is that one day every person will see that "beautiful bush" situated in front of a decrepit, abandoned building. This book is a product of your guidance, teachings and support. For everything you've done and everything you continue to do, I am so very grateful to call you my mother.

To my father, Rich (Dicky). You taught me the values of hard work, selflessness and perseverance. A salesman by day and computer programmer by night during the early stages of your career, you refused to let life's hardships steer your course. Your refusal to listen to my excuses or to accept anything less than my best "positive mental attitude" encouraged me to figure out a solution to every problem. The same person that sealed multi-million dollar telecommunications deals also wired houses for those in need around the community for a six-pack of Pabst Blue Ribbon. My brother Jordan said it best, "Dad is the only person I know that could toast champagne to a bunch of snobs in tuxedos in one room and chug a PBR with a crew of blue collar workers in an adjacent room without missing a beat." For all of these qualities, I thank you.

To my oldest brother, Jared. Your kindness and sincere appreciation for the good in everything encourages me to view the world differently than I am accustomed to. Your feedback and support continues to encourage me and inspire me in ways you probably aren't aware. You frequently comment that "you have no idea how I stay so positive and continue to pursue a career in an industry cluttered with corruption and difficult outcomes." Your support and friendship is a big part of it.

To my older brother, Jordan. You encourage me to stick with my plan during the tough times and serve as an excellent sounding board for my new ideas and career pursuits. You taught me to take risks by limiting the little things I constantly worry about that quite frankly aren't worth worrying about. Most of the time you are right. Your business intelligence is something I admire and value almost daily.

To my clients. Thank you! For believing in me. For staying with me regardless of the circumstances. And, most importantly, for entrusting me with your career. This journey is better served when both parties are pursuing their individual dreams. I don't accomplish mine unless you realize yours, which motivates me to succeed. To all of my clients, past, present and future, my hope is that we remain close years after your professional football careers come to an end.

To my contributors. *From Mascot To Agent* wouldn't have been possible without you. What makes this collaboration great is the level of detail and personal involvement behind each of your stories. There is no one better equipped to talk about a specific role in an industry than someone occupying that role. This book provides an avenue for aspiring professionals to obtain this information, mostly in part because of your contributions. I thank you for your involvement, friendship, and support during this entire process.

To my grandparents. Vicky Erchick. At the age of 90, you still remind me that life should be fun. Your sense of humor and enjoyment of life is an inspiration to our entire family. Ohio U's Beer Pong Granny will be a memory I will never forget. Ralph and Gunhild Hunt (deceased). More so than anything, you taught me the value of hard work. You pursued your own passions and opened your own business. The lessons instilled in your children and grandchildren carry on to this day. Jay Erchick (deceased). You taught me to stay humble, take care of business, and refrain from complaining. I see these qualities in my mother and her siblings. This is something I need to work on, and you served as a perfect example.

To my extended family and friends. Family is an integral part of everything I do. Every member of my family has contributed to my career and/or this book in some way, shape or form, but some have gone the extra mile and deserve specific recognition. To my cousin John Kuceyeski. Stay true to your passion. "Tough times don't last; tough people do." I am proud of everything you've accomplished and grateful for everything you've helped me accomplish. Stick with your passion. Others won't. To my cousin, Kristen Kuceyeski. Your friendship is something I will cherish forever. Your insight into writing is something for which my readers will be grateful! While the days of singing Jackson 5 in your bedroom are long gone, the friendship that was created during these moments will last forever. To Erin Kuceyeski Lynch and Britt Kuceyeski Burns and families. You housed me when I lived out of a box on my travels and fed me in between meetings in your respective cities. I can't thank you enough.

To my friend, Terri Pastorino. When I was a young kid, you promised me that if I ever worked for the 49ers, I would have a free place to stay in Santa Clara. You were one of my first phone calls when I received my offer. And you stayed true to your word. Your willingness to let me stay at your home, eat your food and occupy your time is reflective of your selflessness and kindness that so many benefit from. You made my opportunity with the 49ers and the start of my career in the sports industry possible. Thank you!

To my editor. You decided to take on this project despite the fact that I had a limited background as a professional writer. Your perspective, insights and recommendations changed the structure of my book and refined the content. This book wouldn't have been possible without your involvement. Thank you!

To those I may have missed. Thank you!

NOTES

[i] Justin Hunt, Why Single Is Better: The Implications of a Multi-Entity Ruling on Revenue Sharing and the NFL Salary Cap, 10 Va. Sports & Ent. L.J. 17 (2010).

[ii] Justin Hunt, To Share Or Not To Share: Revenue Sharing Structures in Professional Sports, 13 Tex. Rev. Ent. & Sports L. 139 (2012).

[iii] This perception has changed recently when Eric Fisher and Khalil Mack were drafted in the first round of the 2013 and 2014 NFL drafts, respectfully.

[iv] Compensatory Draft Picks are awarded to clubs at the end of rounds three through seven based on a formula that takes into account the number of players a team loses in free agency. Historically, the number of Compensatory Draft Picks awarded was limited to 32 and the picks could not be traded. This is expected to change beginning in 2017.

[v] The exclusion of these revenues from the players' share incentivized stadium improvements. The owners didn't have to split the revenues, which contributed to the stadium boom that occurred in the 2000s.

[vi] Skip Sauer, "Cowboys Stadium Financing," *The Sports Economist*, accessed on July 11, 2010. An Auction Rate Security (ARS) is a debt or preferred equity security that has an interest rate that is periodically re-set through auctions, typically every week to every four weeks. These are generally structures as bonds with long-time maturities or preferred shares.

[vii] The American Bar Association, "ABA National Lawyer Population Survey," accessed on December 16, 2015.

[viii] Baseball Almanac, "Oakland Athletics Attendance Data," accessed on February 15, 2015.

[ix] Baseball Almanac, "Oakland Athletics Attendance Data," accessed on February 15, 2015.

[x] College Sports Scholarships, "NCAA Restricted Earnings Coach Rule," accessed on March 28, 2013. Restricted earnings positions were created by the NCAA's Cost Reduction Committee in 1991. This essentially limited the earnings of graduate assistants to no more than $16,000 a year. This backfired on the NCAA when it lost a class action lawsuit resulting in a multi-million dollar judgment against the NCAA in a lower-court decision.

[xi] Beta tapes, also referred to as Betamax, were a videocassette magnetic tape recording format that pre-dated VHS tapes. This technology ceased production in 2002, but became obsolete long before this cease-production date.

[xii] The Official Site of the Los Angeles Dodgers, accessed on March 10, 2016.

[xiii] Sunnucks, Mike, "Diamondbacks value has nearly doubled in past decade," accessed on April 10, 2014.

[xiv] Jayson Stark, "MLB's Next Commissioner?" access on May 26, 2014.

[xv] Judy Battista, "Eagles' Spree Was Years In The Making," accessed on June 16, 2014.

[xvi] A Credited Season is earned under the NFL's Collective Bargaining Agreement for each season a player is on, or should have been on, full pay status for a total of three or more regular season games, excluding certain player designations. The number of credited seasons determines the benefits and, in some instances, the salary available to an NFL player. This is different than an Accrued Season, which determines a player's free agency status and accrues if a player is on full pay status for a total of six or more games, excluding certain player designations.

[xvii] E. Scott Reckard, "Steinberg to Sell Firm for $120 Million," accessed on March 15, 2016.

[xviii] The New York Times, "Falk Is Bought Out by SFX," accessed on April 12, 2016.

[xix] In the NFL, a player's Paragraph 5 salary is the base compensation a player receives if he makes a team's 53-man roster and is on the active/inactive list during the regular season. This amount under the contract is paid as it is earned over the course of

the season. Other compensation terms include signing bonuses, roster bonuses, reporting bonuses, workout bonuses and incentive payments, among others.

[xx] Andrew Brandt, "An agent's life isn't all glamour," accessed on May 11, 2016.

CPSIA information can be obtained
at www.ICGtesting.com
Printed in the USA
LVOW12s0058050917

547552LV00001B/66/P